Postcards, Translators and Esperanto Pioneers

Postcards, Translators and Esperanto Pioneers

An Alternative History of International Communication

Guilherme Fians,
Bernhard Struck and
Claire Taylor

UNIVERSITY OF LONDON PRESS

Available to purchase in print or download
for free at https://uolpress.co.uk

First published 2025 by
University of London Press
Senate House, Malet St, London WC1E 7HU

A CIP catalogue record for this book is available from The British Library.

ISBN 978-1-914477-87-4 (hardback)
ISBN 978-1-914477-88-1 (paperback)
ISBN 978-1-914477-91-1 (.epub)
ISBN 978-1-914477-90-4 (.pdf)
ISBN 978-1-914477-89-8 (.html)

DOI https://doi.org/10.63674/wujq4585

Cover image: Zeppelin with inscription "Esperanto", 1920.
Österreichische Nationalbibliothek.

Cover design for University of London Press by Nicky Borowiec.
Book design by Nigel French.
Text set by Westchester Publishing Services UK
in Source Sans Pro, designed by Paul D. Hunt.

Contents

List of figures

Note from the authors

Since this book largely addresses multilingualism and translation, it is important to begin with some considerations on language.

All translations from Esperanto, French and German into English are our own, unless otherwise noted. Most translated quotes appear alongside the original in the main text. For lengthier quotes, we have decided to keep the original Esperanto – and some French – in the main text, to give readers a flavour of Esperanto and of the multilingual exchanges that our book focuses on. Translations are provided in the footnotes.

References abbreviated as 'John Beveridge Collection' in footnotes refer to documents held at the University of St Andrews Special Collections, which served as our primary archive for source material.

Acknowledgements

Some books begin being written by accident. This book certainly did, but it was a happy accident. It began with one of those lucky dips in the archives that historians need here and there. Yet at times these come unexpectedly. Working on the early Esperanto language community from a transnational perspective, Bernhard Struck had been to archives in Britain, Austria, Germany and Czechia. And while Esperanto – as this book shows – was nearly everywhere in Europe around 1910, something was missing: a rich personal archive that could showcase an individual's life in, with and around the language.

Returning from archives in Prague in 2020, Bernhard wondered: why not type 'Esperanto' into the University of St Andrews' catalogue? And there it was: thousands of entries of books, manuscript sources and the unexpected, unexplored John Beveridge Collection – a truly unique archive in its entirety.

But this was not an isolated happy accident. Bernhard had the fortune to meet Guilherme Fians at the University of Manchester in 2019, when Bernhard gave his first talk ever on Esperanto. Bernhard and Guilherme stayed in touch and discovered their mutual interests around Esperanto, language politics, communication technologies and knowledge production. Through pandemic-style Zoom meetings between Brazil and Scotland, they submitted a joint grant application to the Leverhulme Trust in 2020 – and got it.

And the final happy accident and missing puzzle piece was Claire Taylor. A second-year history and English student at the time, Claire approached Bernhard in 2020 inquiring about research internships. Bringing together Bernhard's findings about Esperanto and Claire's interest in women's history, they applied for funding from the Laidlaw Foundation – and got it.

So here we were, an unexpected team of two historians and a social anthropologist, plenty of archival sources and a shared enthusiasm for languages and transnational history. We decided to fully dig into the John Beveridge Collection together between 2022 and 2025. Based on what we found in the archives, the three of us had fun curating an exhibition on language, media and globalisation at the Wardlaw Museum, in St Andrews, in April–May 2023. Following the extremely positive interest and attention our exhibition received, we realised the full potential of the material we had at hand and began writing this book. We hope the pages that follow will captivate and surprise our readers as much as this collection fascinated us.

But this book would not have come into being without the generous support we received from a number of colleagues, friends and institutions. We would like to thank the Leverhulme Trust for funding Bernhard and Guilherme's joint project 'Sharing Knowledge in Esperanto: From Expert to Participatory Cultures, 1900/2000', which allowed us to work on this book. We would also like to express our gratitude to the Laidlaw Foundation, which funded Claire's participation in the project, and our colleagues from the School of History at the University of St Andrews – where the three of us were once based – for supporting our adventures in research.

Introduction: building worlds with words

Ludwik Lejzer Zamenhof was born in 1859 in the city of Białystok, then in western tsarist Russia. Growing up in a Jewish family in a city that gathered speakers of German, Russian, Polish and Yiddish, he came to perceive multilingualism as an obstacle preventing mutual understanding among people from different national, ethnic and linguistic backgrounds. Seeking to overcome nationalist rivalries and bring humankind together, Zamenhof constructed an international auxiliary language in the 1880s. Initially labelled *Internacia Lingvo* (International Language), it later became known as Esperanto, following the pseudonym *Dr Esperanto* under which Zamenhof launched his language project. On the opposite side of Europe, in 1857 – two years before Zamenhof's birth – John Beveridge was born in Ayr, a town on the west coast of Scotland. Growing up in an ordinary, middle-class family, John Beveridge later became a Presbyterian clergyman and moved to Dundee, on Scotland's east coast, where he lived for most of his life.

While Ludwik Zamenhof drew on his language skills covering Polish, Russian, Yiddish, French, German, Latin, ancient Greek and English to design his constructed language in 1887, John Beveridge was then a monolingual English speaker, living in a predominantly monolingual setting.[1] Whereas Ludwik Zamenhof became known worldwide and has had his life analysed in a number of biographies, John Beveridge was mostly forgotten by history.[2] Given the striking differences in terms of nationality, occupation, religion and linguistic background between these two men contemporary to each other, it may be hard to imagine that they would ever have something to say to each other. However, in 1910, Ludwik Zamenhof sent a postcard to John Beveridge. The postcard was in Esperanto, the language that the latter learned in the early 1900s, when he became part of the first generation of speakers of this constructed language.

In this book, we take the postcards written in Esperanto and exchanged between these two men as an entry point for understanding how international communication functioned in the early twentieth century. Our guiding question is: what might we find by analysing international communication and globalisation through the lens of Esperanto and postcards, rather than through the commonplace focus on the late twentieth-century use of English and social media? An attention to language creation enables us to explore how constructed languages – alongside communication technologies such as international postal services – played a key role in shaping the early waves of globalisation that preceded the dominance of global English.

Two men, one language

As the creator of a rather widespread language, it is no surprise that Ludwik Zamenhof has been the subject of numerous scholarly works. John Beveridge, by contrast, did not become known for any particular achievement. Why should someone write – or, for that matter, read – a book that largely revolves around John Beveridge?

Living in Dundee with his Australian-born wife and four Scottish-born children, John Beveridge (1857–1943) was a Presbyterian clergyman, avid reader, enthusiastic beekeeper and someone deeply curious about world affairs. Among his many personal interests were the Norwegian language, customs and history – interests that led him to improve his Norwegian skills with the help of Esperanto-speaking contacts and to visit Norway several times. He also travelled to the 1912 Universal Congress of Esperanto in Kraków. Yet, before these travels, John Beveridge pursued a largely provincial lifestyle, going from his parish back home at the end of each day. In those years prior to his journeys abroad, the city of Dundee served as a constant reminder of the world 'out there' and all it had to offer.

In 1901, the RRS Discovery set sail from Dundee – where it was built – on its first intercontinental expedition to the Antarctic. Around the same year, the Port of Dundee was bustling with ships from around the globe coming on a daily basis to commercialise their products. The many spinning mills and power-loom factories in the city accounted for workers from different parts of Scotland and Europe, as well as busy export routes involving the

Mediterranean, Australia, the United States, South America and the West Indies. In addition to these businesses, the jute trade was responsible for a significant proportion of Dundee's internationality. The raw jute was imported from Bengal in colonial India, processed in Scottish mills and then exported to places like the United States and Brazil. The trade and manufacturing of jute attracted people from different nationalities to Dundee.[3]

Around 1900, Dundee was one of the major port cities in Britain. Yet the city was not what one would consider to be a popular cultural hub, and not everyone in Dundee participated directly in the city's maritime trade. John Beveridge, for one, did not. However, the constant buzz around jute, whaling and shipbuilding was tangible. Likewise, not every foreign sailor arriving in Scotland spoke English. However, there were other means – and languages – available to those in Dundee who wanted to participate in international flows and get to know people from other nationalities. Around 1906, to go beyond his Scottish milieu, John Beveridge and two of his daughters – Heather and Lois Beveridge – learned Esperanto. In the following years, they used it to meet and exchange correspondence with people from across the world. This is how John Beveridge would later encounter Ludwik Zamenhof, as well as many other fellow Esperanto speakers. This encounter raises the question as to why someone would come up with a language from scratch – and, what is more, why someone other than Zamenhof, from another country, would invest time and effort in learning such a constructed language.

This is what this book is about. What happened to a language, created in a specific place and context, when it travelled to different places and contexts? How did an international auxiliary language – rather than more consolidated, hegemonic languages such as French or English – emerge as an entryway for ordinary people to experience internationalism in practice? What kinds of grassroots internationalism could 'global' languages afford people such as the Beveridge family? And, finally, at a time when steamships, international postal services and the telephone were setting the pace of the waves of globalisation in place in the early twentieth century, what role could language play in this increasingly international(ist) scenario?

As much as we know about languages and technologies used for international communication, we know far less about the everyday lives of Esperanto speakers and the functioning of this language community on the ground. By zooming in on Dundee and the Beveridge family, this book recasts the lives of ordinary Esperanto speakers which – as revealed in their postcards, networks and participation in congresses – were anything but ordinary. In doing so, we narrate one among many alternative histories of international communication, using as our entryways not French or English, not the television or the internet, but Esperanto and postcards.

A linguistic solution to a geopolitical problem

At first glance, it may seem odd that many people have communicated, formulated ideas and established relationships using words and grammatical structures that originated at a single person's desk. Yet Esperanto had – and continues to have – a raison d'être: it was created as a solution to a pressing problem.

The late nineteenth and early twentieth centuries constituted critical moments in the history of globalisation. The decades labelled *La Belle Époque* in western Europe saw considerable technological advancement, with the telephone gradually replacing the telegraph, the development of electric and diesel locomotives, the flight of the first aeroplane and the popularisation of international postal services.[4] These technological transformations, on the one hand, nurtured certain European perceptions of modernity, which came to be epitomised by the Universal Exhibitions. Regularly held since 1851, these Exhibitions featured national pavilions through which countries competed to present their cultural and technological achievements to the world.[5]

On the other hand, these technological developments helped expose the unequal power relations that Europe established with other continents. Combined with how colonialism and imperialism expanded European hegemony to the African and Asian continents,[6] these geopolitical and technological transformations gave ordinary Europeans more reasons to seek ways to communicate and travel across borders, either to explore Europe's overseas territories or to participate in colonialist endeavours.[7] These elements underpinning the early twentieth-century waves of globalisation also reinforced the rhetoric according to which modernity was a European commodity to be exported. This is what justified, for instance, the many attempts led by governments and scientists to standardise language use – through the teaching of hegemonic languages in colonial spaces – as well as scientific vocabulary and units of measurement. Faced with the fast-increasing reach of European people, goods, values and ideas across the globe, standardisation took shape through a series of efforts to simplify the world before it became too complex.[8]

Against this background, the growing circulation of people, goods and ideas imposed a question: in which language would a Scottish journalist write a postcard to a French or Romanian colleague, or which language would a German merchant speak upon disembarking from a steamship in the West Indies?

This increasingly integrated world revealed and reinforced several forms of injustice and power imbalance. Not by chance, this moment was also characterised by tensions involving exclusionary nationalism, mass migration and imperialist oppressions of all sorts.[9] Amidst political, economic and cultural imperialism, linguistic imperialism also gained prominence, as imperialism and nation-building entailed by default the imposition of the coloniser's hegemonic national language over speakers of minoritised languages.[10] Once acknowledged that a more integrated world depended not only on communication and transportation technologies but also languages, the quest for an international auxiliary language gained traction.

At the turn of the twentieth century, several proposals to facilitate international communication emerged, mainly encouraging the use of French and English as standardising global languages. However, the use of these as lingua francas often faced resistance from nationalists and anti-imperialists who refused to embrace the hegemonic language of another nation-state.[11] Aiming to address this matter, an alternative proposal took shape: what if international communication was based on a constructed language – non-national in its own right and, therefore, free of nationalisms? Hundreds of such language projects emerged in the period labelled 'the battle of artificial languages'. Among them, Esperanto stood out, having gathered over two million speakers by the beginning of the century and enduring to this day, more than 135 years on.[12]

Designed on Ludwik Zamenhof's desk in Warsaw, Esperanto draws heavily on Romance, Germanic and Slavic languages.[13] Using the Latin script, it reads, sounds and feels familiar to speakers of European languages, which helped its diffusion in both European and imperial spaces. Yet, the dissemination of this language owed significantly to how Esperanto was from the outset a language with a cause.

Zamenhof did not envisage his language project as a prospective replacement for the world's languages. Rather, he intended Esperanto to be used as a 'bridge of words' to connect people who would otherwise be unable to communicate.[14] As an international auxiliary language, Esperanto belonged to no single ethnic or national group. It was no one's first language – so it could be anyone's second language. Zamenhof made this principle clear by encouraging all Esperanto speakers to contribute to the ongoing development of the language's vocabulary.[15] In short, Zamenhof and the early generation of Esperanto speakers conveyed Esperanto as a collaborative, co-constructed language, to be used with the goal of creating a common ground on which potentially anyone is welcome. By stepping outside the linguistic comfort zone of one's first language, people would use this international auxiliary language as a meeting point from where they could share what they have in common as fellow human beings and learn from each other's differences as citizens of different nation-states.

Throughout the long twentieth century, other international auxiliary languages were created. This included Volapük – Esperanto's predecessor – whose language community prospered for a short period in Europe before being engulfed by the rapid growth of Esperanto. This landscape also included Ido and Novial – Esperanto's short-lived successors – which failed to get off the ground and develop fully fledged language communities. Such a quest for a common language for international communication was also on the radar of internationalist bodies, such as the Delegation for the Adoption of an International Auxiliary Language, created within the framework of the 1900 Universal Exhibition in Paris.[16] Additionally, in 1922, the newly established League of Nations formed a commission to discuss the introduction of a constructed language in school curricula.[17] Such debates also gained relevance in the US in 1924, with the establishment of the International Auxiliary Language Association.[18]

Babbling first words, crafting alternative worlds: on constructing a language and a community

In 1887, Zamenhof launched a booklet in Russian with the basics of his language project. Nicknamed *Unua Libro* (First Book), this booklet was immediately published in other languages, with its Polish, French and German versions appearing in the later months of 1887, as well as an English version in 1888. These versions were later compiled in a multilingual edition in the five above-mentioned languages under the title *Fundamento de Esperanto*.[19] With an introduction justifying the need for such a language – followed by an abridged grammar, language learning exercises and a dictionary – this booklet set the ground for Esperanto to take shape and attract its first speakers, primarily in Russian-speaking territories. Yet it did not take long for Esperanto groups to begin mushrooming across Europe and beyond at the turn of the century, which invites us to consider the particularities of this language and of the community that developed around it.[20]

In this regard, the term conventionally used to refer to speakers of a given language who recognise it as a group-forming element is *speech community*.[21] However, Esperanto contrasts with most so-called 'natural languages' in how its speakers tend to prioritise its written form over the spoken. To account for this particularity, we have adopted the term *language community* to reflect the emic term *Esperantujo* (Esperanto community, literally 'the container of Esperanto'). The term *language community* not only captures the idea that Esperanto speakers share a common language – as in a speech community – but also highlights the way they gather around language-based practices, such as translating into Esperanto, debating linguistic minutiae, and organising Esperanto gatherings – practices akin to those found in communities of practice.[22] Additionally, since Esperanto was initially created in written form and only effectively spoken when a second person – other than Zamenhof – learned it, this pre-eminence of written over spoken language is also evident in Esperanto's prevailing use through correspondence in its first decades.[23]

While several scholars refer to the assemblage of Esperanto speakers interchangeably as the *Esperanto community* and the *Esperanto movement*,[24] we choose the label *community*. This term underscores that promoting the global use of this language through activism – what one may expect from a language movement such as, for instance, the Basque or the Corsican movement[25] – may not be the primary way most Esperanto speakers engage with the language. Along the same lines, we choose the label *Esperanto speaker*, instead of *Esperantist*, to emphasise an engagement that lies primarily in the language, not being necessarily connected to the internationalist ideals that nurtured the Esperanto movement at the time.

Unlike the way languages and their communities of speakers customarily develop hand in hand, Esperanto provides a scenario in which the language takes precedence over its community. To consolidate such a constructed language, its early speakers had to create reasons for other people to feel attracted to the language. In addition to consolidating a literary corpus and a language community,[26] this groundwork also involved linking with other causes the loosely defined forms of language-based internationalism associated with Esperanto.

In the eastern part of Europe, Esperanto was first embraced by pacifists and Tolstoyans, who perceived the language as a tool to oppose the ethno-linguistic factionalism so prominent in tsarist Russia.[27] In the western part of Europe, primarily in France, the idealistic perception of Esperanto as a harmonising, peace-promoting tool came to coexist with Esperanto's pragmatic use as a language that epitomised the modernity of *La Belle Époque*. With nineteen Esperanto courses taking place simultaneously in Paris alone in 1902–3,[28] the language attracted the attention primarily of intellectuals, scientists and members of the middle classes in the country. For one reason or another, internationally driven publics across Europe learned and used Esperanto in large numbers, combining the language with emerging communication and transport technologies to build cross-border networks and establish personal ties, as well as exchange and produce political, scientific and lay knowledge.

Despite having never become the world's lingua franca, Esperanto constitutes a remarkable phenomenon from a historical, sociological and linguistic point of view, given the way so many people have voluntarily opted for learning and using a non-compulsory language for diverse purposes over the twentieth and twenty-first centuries. It is not surprising, then, that a number of researchers have explored aspects of the Esperanto language, movement and community.

In general lines, the bountiful scholarly literature on linguistic aspects of Esperanto centres on language planning, vocabulary development and themes that inquire whether Esperanto is a language like any other or an exceptional one.[29] Meanwhile, scholarship on literature has approached the particular features (if any) of literature produced originally in Esperanto, as well as translation and the use of Esperanto to make literary works in minority or national languages available to an international readership.[30]

Among historians and sociologists, the key monographs concerning Esperanto explore primarily the early decades of the language, when the language community and movement were getting off the ground and finding ways of connecting this newly created language with broader societal demands and struggles. These studies systematically map out these developments from the perspective of the key spaces and actors of this story: analysing the battle of artificial languages in late nineteenth and early twentieth-century Europe, when Esperanto emerged alongside other constructed languages competing for global spread and international recognition;[31] exploring the links between Esperanto and left-wing activism as the language was embraced by pacifists, communists and anarchists;[32] and investigating the persecution of international-minded people, among which Esperanto speakers, by totalitarian regimes in Europe and Asia.[33]

Other sociological and anthropological approaches, in turn, have centred on delineating the constitution of such a diverse and geographically dispersed community throughout the twentieth century, as well as the shapes taken by this language community in the twenty-first century amidst the emergence of digital technologies.[34] A number of biographies complement this scholarship by portraying personal and contextual traits of Ludwik Lejzer Zamenhof,[35] as well as of other prominent actors in Esperanto's history, such as Ludwik Zamenhof's daughter Lidia Zamenhof[36] and a key advocate for Esperanto among proletarians and anti-nationalist activists, Eugène Lanti.[37]

However, the breadth of Esperanto as a topic for scholarly research also substantiates the shortcomings of this historiography. First, despite Esperanto being a wholeheartedly transnational phenomenon, the vast majority of studies on it tend to focus on national settings, analysing the spread of Esperanto in bounded national spaces such as tsarist (later Soviet) Russia, France and Spain. These are the places where Esperanto gained more prominence in twentieth-century Europe, which justifies the foci of these studies. However, by taking national borders for granted, these country-centred approaches leave out the most striking trait of this language, namely its use to forge cross-border connections and networks.

Second, an attention to the key locations where Esperanto gained visibility cast aside the many other people and places at the margins of this emerging Esperanto-speaking world. In cities like Paris in 1903 or Warsaw in 1907, Esperanto speakers likely had little trouble finding fellow speakers, attending weekly classes or joining local clubs. Their motivation to learn the language may well have stemmed from the multilingual and multicultural character of their cities, where Esperanto offered an alternative entry point into an increasingly interconnected world.

This, however, was far from the reality for those interested in Esperanto in places like Dundee, Scotland, or Harmanli, Bulgaria, in the early twentieth century – places that were neither considered transnational hubs nor featured a well-developed and institutionalised local Esperanto-speaking landscape. How, then, did people in such settings materialise and make sense of their interest in this international auxiliary language? What kind of internationalism could 'global' languages afford people such as the Beveridge family? Unpacking how Esperanto serves as a bridge connecting nowhere to anywhere, we explore how these speakers found value in learning and using Esperanto from semi-rural settings in Scotland or Bulgaria around 1910.

First stop: the Beveridge family

This book seeks to dislocate the history of Esperanto and reinsert it in transnational history. Departing from how most scholarly works have centred on key multilingual hubs or on prominent actors in this language community and movement in the first half of the twentieth century, our focus on the Beveridge family provides a rather marginal gateway into the Esperanto phenomenon. From perspectives such as John's, Lois's and Heather Beveridge's, how would one gain access to Esperanto language learning materials and effectively use the language when very few people in one's surroundings seemed to share this interest? Activities such as swimming, gardening, playing a musical instrument or cooking can be done individually. However, using a language is a conversational practice and, as with any communicative venture, is collective in its own right. What would be the point of learning Esperanto if you know of no one other than your family members who could use it with you?[38] A close look at the interests and uses of this language by John, Lois and Heather Beveridge allows us to follow the first steps of the consolidation and institutionalisation of Esperanto on the east coast of Scotland, where using the language entailed not only learning it but also creating contexts whereby this language could be spoken and written.

Rooted in this not so international and not particularly multilingual corner of Scotland, John Beveridge used Esperanto to establish transnational networks, from which he discussed topics ranging from Christianity and Scandinavian history to beekeeping. Additionally, he published magazine articles in Esperanto on Christianity, delivered sermons and contributed to the first Esperanto translation of the New Testament. And, as Esperanto was a family affair in the Beveridge household, he was not entirely alone in this endeavour. Two of his daughters also exchanged postcards, helped found the Scottish Esperanto Federation, taught Esperanto, produced scholarly articles in the language and attended international congresses abroad. Bridging their world with others', their words reached faraway places, helping to build a geographically dispersed community whose members/speakers are potentially everywhere, but concentrated nowhere.

There is very little on the lives of those at the fringes – and yet, in many ways, at the heart – of the Esperanto phenomenon. Individuals like the Beveridges were the backbone of a vigorous language community, even though they did not live in Warsaw, Paris, Barcelona or Berlin, nor attended the first international Esperanto congress held in 1905. While existing biographies of Ludwik Zamenhof, Lidia Zamenhof and Eugène Lanti focus on the key achievements of prominent Esperanto speakers, turning instead to John, Lois and Heather Beveridge will enable us to zoom in on the everyday lives of people who were not full-time Esperanto speakers – without losing sight of this family's other interests and occupations, as well as gender and societal roles. In this regard, this book is not *about* the Beveridge family. Rather, it is a book written *around* the Beveridge family, which takes them as figureheads to account for an alternative approach to the history of international communication.[39]

Few archives from early Esperanto speakers have been made public or survived time. By contrast, the well-documented but yet unexplored Beveridge family enables us to reconstitute the lives of some of these individuals. Shortly before his death, in 1943, John Beveridge expressed the wish to have the bulk of his letters, postcards, papers and books donated to the University of St Andrews. This archive constitutes one of the most complete collections with information about individual lives of Esperanto speakers of the time. Starting from the St Andrews' John Beveridge Collection, we followed paper trails this family left through language learning exercise books, minutes of Esperanto club meetings, translations, personal notes, magazine collections, registers of attendance of Esperanto congresses, newspaper articles and books held also by the Department of Planned Languages at the Austrian National Library, Edinburgh's National Library of Scotland, the Local History Centre at Dundee's Central Library and the records of Scotland Censuses, among other primary sources that revealed new facets of our curious and unique actors.

These archives provide an understanding of cross-border exchanges amidst global French and before global English – an understanding that often escapes the mainstream historiography of Esperanto and international communication. By (re)writing and analysing this history from the margins – such as from the connections between Scotland and Bulgaria that we explore in Chapter 1 – we are able to highlight how the perceived marginality of certain places drove people to seek linguistic means of feeling integrated in transnational networks.

In speaking of margins, we do not intend to invoke a simplistic dichotomy of centre versus margins/periphery. First, Esperanto developed differently across various locations at the time. Second, a not-so-central city in Scotland cannot epitomise all possible meanings of marginality. After all, given how international auxiliary languages emerged as a European phenomenon, would not spaces on other continents more typically constitute 'margins'? Dundee was one among numerous not-so-central places in the history of languages and communication technologies. As such, it served as a stage for a particular articulation of Esperanto's history – one that did not necessarily centre on Zamenhof or the first international congress.

Similarly, it took decades for a sizeable portion of the population of Dundee to have access to telephones and for the invention of the aeroplane to gain relevance to Dundonians. This may lead us to question: to what extent is it fair to refer to this period as *La Belle Époque*?[40] This *époque* may not have been forcefully *belle* for people in these locations. In this regard, the approach we propose here aims precisely at giving visibility to people who did not engage with languages and technologies the same way as those in hubs such as Paris, Prague or Chicago. Ultimately, Dundee as a place may be marginal but not atypical. The combination of an individual's life (John Beveridge) and a somewhere place (Dundee) allows us to account for an alternative history of international communication across spaces and scales from the individual, familial and local to the national and international.[41]

Ultimately, examining how John Beveridge established contacts with Norwegian clergymen, how Lois Beveridge taught languages, and how Heather Beveridge produced academic articles offers a novel perspective on Esperanto's growing popularity around the turn of the century and reveals how languages and technologies were used to engender alternative forms of modernity at the time.

Road map: where languages and communication technologies can take us

Starting our journey from John, Lois and Heather Beveridge, this book aims to bring readers to as many places as Esperanto and postcards brought this Scottish family. To do so, the pages that follow recast the history of languages and technologies, exploring international communication from a perspective at once individual – from the Beveridges' perspective – and transnational – from the connections they built.

Chapter 1 delves into John Beveridge's collection of more than fifty letters and postcards sent to Dundee from locations such as Harmanli, Kymi, Kutná Hora, Nový Bydžov and Superaguy. This chapter illustrates the breadth of the networks that people built to exchange information about Esperanto life, translation, the latest literature and non-Esperanto-related topics. These postcards allow us to reconstruct international communication through focusing on emerging languages and communication technologies viewed from the standpoint of one of several 'marginal' Esperanto speakers – thus moving beyond the usual narratives around Zamenhof's achievements, major Esperanto associations and international congresses.

Chapter 2 situates Esperanto in Scotland, and Scotland in the international Esperanto landscape. From the traces of local Esperanto clubs and associations, we explore how the Beveridges and other Scotland-based Esperanto speakers attempted to put Scotland on Esperanto's map via the creation of Esperanto clubs in lesser-known places like Montrose, Arbroath and Linlithgow, the establishment of the Scottish Esperanto Federation, and an attempt to hold the 1915 Universal Congress of Esperanto in Edinburgh. By regularly organising local meetings, offering language classes and inviting foreign participants to local congresses, these Scottish individuals and institutions helped materialise this language community in its early decades by creating contexts for Esperanto to be effectively spoken.

Chapter 3 deconstructs international auxiliary languages as a male-centric phenomenon. Given that gender has been a systematically neglected aspect of Esperanto's history, the Beveridge daughters – Lois and her teaching of the language, and Heather and her translation of chemistry journal articles – act as examples of how family networks and women's language teaching were integral to the pre-war growth of Esperanto. This chapter also considers the roles that various Dundee and Edinburgh women doctors, teachers and journalists held in local Esperanto clubs and abroad when they travelled to attend Universal Congresses of Esperanto in Antwerp (1911) and Kraków (1912).

Chapter 4 explores the first translation of the Bible into Esperanto to examine the processes of language creation and community-building on the ground. While Zamenhof translated the Old Testament from Hebrew, John Beveridge became part of the team that translated the New Testament from Ancient Greek. However, it was challenging to coin Esperanto terms for abstractions such as 'grace' and 'joy' so that these terms could be understood by Jews and Christians from diverse countries, denominations and linguistic backgrounds. While disagreements around vocabulary development unfolded between Jews and Christians, these translators were also developing Esperanto-speaking interfaith networks and forging vocabulary to refer to things not initially named by Zamenhof.

The conclusion argues for small-scale, empirical approaches to understanding transnational history in the making, moving beyond grand narratives that recount history from the standpoint of empires, governments and key political actors.[42] Ultimately, this book explores how languages and technologies substantiate the ways we build worlds through words. John, Lois and Heather Beveridge used postcards, steamships and Esperanto to join transnational flows – which were just a few among many languages and technologies available to them at the time.

Research on internationalism and multilingualism tends to focus on the mainstream spaces where these world phenomena gained ground – from the Universal Exhibitions to the Olympic Games and the United Nations. By contrast, cross-border correspondence in Esperanto reverberates a form of grassroots internationalism that illustrates how ordinary people were effectively experiencing the technologies and values that underpinned modernity and the early twentieth-century waves of globalisation.

Writing around John, Lois and Heather Beveridge allows for an overview of a deeply entangled world around 1900 from a 'marginal' perspective and place: Esperanto and/in Dundee. 'Globalisation' tends to direct our thoughts to the late twentieth and early twenty-first centuries – and rightly so, given the technological and commercial changes in recent decades. Yet, however challenging diachronic comparisons across a century might be, both the 1900s and the 2000s are characterised by rapid changes that spurred both globalisation and its backlashes, including 'crises' framed in terms of nationalism, war and mass migration. While this book does not engage with these topics in greater detail, zooming in on this family allows for a glimpse into the lives of hopeful and curious people who sought to embrace the potential futures and opportunities the 1900s offered – with and through Esperanto, which in itself reveals something of its time. After all, this is what 'Esperanto' means: the one who hopes. Going beyond a study of a few individuals, these pages are written in the hopeful and internationalist spirit that nurtures Esperanto and that equips us to flesh out the feelings, hopes and life projects at stake.

Notes

1 Brigid O'Keeffe, 'An International Language for an Empire of Humanity: L. L. Zamenhof and the Imperial Russian Origins of Esperanto'. *East European Jewish Affairs* 49, no. 1 (2019): 1–19.

2 Biographies of Zamenhof include Ernest Drezen, *Zamenhof* (Leipzig: Sennacieca Asocio Tutmonda, 1929); Marjorie Boulton, *Zamenhof: Creator of Esperanto* (London: Routledge and Kegan Paul, 1960); Edmond Privat, *La Vivo de Zamenhof* (Tyresö: Inko, 2001); Aleksandr Korzhenkov, *Zamenhof: The Life, Works, and Ideas of the Author of Esperanto* (New York: Mondial, 2010); Walter Żelazny, *Ludwik Zamenhof: Life and Work. Reminiscences* (Białystok: Wydawnictwo Uniwersytetu w Białymstoku, 2020).

3 Jim Tomlinson, *Dundee and the Empire: 'Juteopolis' 1850–1939* (Edinburgh: Edinburgh University Press, 2016); Tara Sethia, 'The Rise of the Jute Manufacturing Industry in Colonial India: A Global Perspective', *Journal of World History* 7, no. 1 (1996): 71–99.

4 See Roland Wenzlhuemer, 'The Dematerialization of Telecommunication: Communication Centres and Peripheries in Europe and the World, 1850–1920', *Journal of Global History* 2, no. 3 (2007), 345–72; Simone Müller, *Wiring the World: The Social and Cultural Creation of Global Telegraph Networks* (New York: Columbia University Press, 2016).

5 Burton Benedict, *The Anthropology of World's Fairs: San Francisco's Panama Pacific International Exposition of 1915* (Berkeley: Lowie Museum of Anthropology and Scolar Press, 1983); John Desmond Bernal, *Science in History, Volume 2: The Scientific and Industrial Revolution* (London: Penguin Books, 1965).

6 Eric Hobsbawm, *The Age of Empire, 1875–1914* (New York: Vintage Books, 1989).

7 Jürgen Osterhammel, *The Transformation of the World: A Global History of the Nineteenth Century* (Princeton: Princeton University Press, 2014).

8 Michael Gordin, *Scientific Babel: How Science Was Done Before and After Global English* (Chicago: University of Chicago Press, 2015).

9 See, for instance, Sebastian Conrad, *Globalisation and the Nation in Imperial Germany* (Cambridge: Cambridge University Press, 2010).

10 See Robert Phillipson, *Linguistic Imperialism* (Oxford: Oxford University Press, 1992).

11 See Phillipson, *Linguistic Imperialism*; Umberto Eco, *The Search for the Perfect Language* (Oxford: Blackwell Publishers, 1995).

12 Roberto Garvía, *Esperanto and Its Rivals: The Struggle for an International Language* (Philadelphia: University of Pennsylvania Press, 2015).

13 John Wells, 'Esperanto', in *Encyclopedia of Language and Linguistics, Volume 4*, ed. Keith Brown (New York: Elsevier, 2006), 223–5.

14 Ludwik Lejzer Zamenhof, 'Paroladoj: Tria Kongreso 1907 en Cambridge', in *Originala Verkaro de L. L. Zamenhof*, ed. Johannes Dietterle (Leipzig: Ferdinand Hirt & Sohn, 1929), 378.

15 Ludwik Lejzer Zamenhof, *Fundamento de Esperanto* (Paris: Hachette, 1905).

16 See Louis Couturat, Otto Jespersen, Richard Lorenz, Leopold Pfaundler Von Hadermur and Wilhelm Ostwald, *International Language and Science: Considerations on the Introduction of an International Language into Science* (London: Constable and Company Limited, 1910); Peter Forster, *The Esperanto Movement: Contributions to the Sociology of Language* (The Hague: Mouton, 1982), 113–27.

17 Inazô Nitobe, 'Esperanto and the Language Question at the League of Nations', in *Al Lingva Demokratio / Towards Linguistic Democracy / Vers La Démocratie Linguistique*, ed. Mark Fettes and Suzanne Bolduc (Rotterdam: Universala Esperanto-Asocio, 1998), 62–78.

18 Mark Fettes, 'The Lady, the Linguists, and the International Language', *Language Problems and Language Planning* 25, no. 2 (2001): 177–84.

19 Zamenhof, *Fundamento de Esperanto*.

20 Garvía, *Esperanto and Its Rivals*.

21 For a comprehensive discussion of the term, see Alessandro Duranti, *Linguistic Anthropology* (Cambridge: Cambridge University Press, 1997), 72–83.

22 Guilherme Fians, *Esperanto Revolutionaries and Geeks: Language Politics, Digital Media and the Making of an International Community* (Cham: Palgrave Macmillan, 2021), 12–14.

23 See John Lyons, *Introduction to Theoretical Linguistics* (Cambridge: Cambridge University Press, 1968), 39.

24 See, for instance, Forster, *The Esperanto Movement*; Garvía, *Esperanto and Its Rivals*.

25 See Jacqueline Urla, 'Ethnic Protest and Social Planning: A Look at Basque Language Revival', *Cultural Anthropology* 3, no. 4 (1988): 379–94; Alexandra Jaffe, *Ideologies in Action: Language Politics on Corsica* (Berlin: Mouton De Gruyter, 1999).

26 Esther Schor, *Bridge of Words: Esperanto and the Dream of a Universal Language* (New York: Metropolitan Books / Henry Holt and Company, 2016).

27 Brigid O'Keeffe, *Esperanto and Languages of Internationalism in Revolutionary Russia* (London: Bloomsbury Academic, 2021).

28 Louis Couturat and Léopold Leau, *Histoire de la Langue Universelle* (Paris: Hachette, 1903), 329.

29 This scholarship came to constitute the core of Interlinguistics, a linguistics subfield focused on the study of constructed languages. For an overview, see Humphrey Tonkin, 'One Hundred Years of Esperanto: A Survey', *Language Problems and Language Planning*, 11, no. 3 (1987): 264–82; Guilherme Fians, 'Bringing Constructed Languages Back to the Debate: The Contributions of Interlinguistics to General Linguistics', *Investigationes Linguisticae* 46 (2022): 43–52; Grant Goodall, 'Constructed Languages', *Annual Review of Linguistics* 9 (2023): 419–37.

30 See, for instance, Ian Richmond, 'Esperanto Literature and the International Reader', in *Aspects of Internationalism: Language and Culture*, ed. Ian Richmond (Lanham, MD: University Press of America, 1993), 103–18; Humphrey Tonkin, 'The Semantics of Invention: Translation into Esperanto', in *The Translator as Mediator of Cultures*, ed. Humphrey Tonkin and Maria Esposito Frank (Amsterdam: John Benjamins, 2010), 169–90.

31 See, for instance, Couturat and Leau, *Histoire de la Langue Universelle*; Louis Couturat and Léopold Leau, *Les Nouvelles Langues Internationales: Suite à l'Histoire de la Langue Universelle* (Paris: Hachette, 1907); Eco, *The Search for the Perfect Language*; Garvía, *Esperanto and Its Rivals*.

32 Roberto Garvía, *Lengua y Utopia: El Movimiento Esperantista en España (1890–1936)* (Granada: Editorial Universidad de Granada, 2021); Javier Alcalde, *Esperanto i Anarquisme: Els Orígens (1887–1907)* (Barcelona: Edicions Malcriàs d'Agràcia, 2022); Guilherme Fians, 'O que falar em esperanto quer dizer: Revisitando políticas prefigurativas, movimentos sociais e as novas esquerdas Mana', *Estudos de Antropologia Social* 29, no. 1 (2023): 1–31.

33 Ulrich Lins, *Dangerous Language: Esperanto under Hitler and Stalin* (London: Palgrave Macmillan, 2016); Ulrich Lins, *Dangerous Language: Esperanto and the Decline of Stalinism* (London: Palgrave Macmillan, 2017); O'Keeffe, *Esperanto and Languages of Internationalism*. For a focus on the persecution of Esperanto speakers in totalitarian regimes in East Asia, see Ulrich Lins, *La Danĝera Lingvo: Esperanto en la Uragano de Persekutoj* (Kyoto: L'Omnibuso, 1973); Ian Rapley, *Green Star Japan: Esperanto and the International Language Question, 1880–1945* (Honolulu: University of Hawaiʻi Press, 2024). For a glimpse of the Brazilian case, see Guilherme Fians, 'TEJO, um maduro movimento de juventude', 240–53, in *O Esperanto Além da Língua*, ed. Fernando Pita and Guilherme Fians (Porto Velho: Temática, 2017), here 38–9.

34 Forster, *The Esperanto Movement*; Nikola Rašić, *La Rondo Familia: Sociologiaj Esploroj en Esperantio* (Pisa: Edistudio, 1994); Irene Caligaris, *Unu Lingvo por Ĉiuj, Unu Lingvo de Neniu Lando: Surkampa Esploro pri la Esperantaj Identecoj* (Pisa: Edistudio, 2021); Schor, *Bridge of Words*; Fians, *Esperanto Revolutionaries and Geeks*.

35 See Drezen, *Zamenhof*; Boulton, *Zamenhof*; Privat, *Vivo de Zamenhof*; Korzhenkov, *Zamenhof*; Żelazny, *Ludwik Zamenhof.*

36 Wendy Heller, *Lidia: The Life of Lidia Zamenhof, the Daughter of Esperanto* (Oxford: George Ronald, 1985).

37 Ed Borsboom, *Vivo de Lanti* (Paris: Sennacieca Asocio Tutmonda, 1976).

38 Hence our preference for referring to *using* rather than *speaking* the language, as we approach a language that is used more frequently in written than in spoken communication. See Fians, *Esperanto Revolutionaries and Geeks.*

39 See Dipesh Chakrabarty, *The Calling of History* (Chicago: University of Chicago Press, 2015), 33, on how to write around a historical actor without turning the account into a biographical study.

40 For a critical approach to the terms used in the periodisation of history, see Ludmilla Jordanova, *History in Practice* (London: Bloomsbury, 2019).

41 See Bernhard Struck, Kate Ferris and Jacques Revel, 'Introduction: Space and Scale in Transnational History', *The International History Review* 33, no. 4 (2011): 573–84. On scales in history, see Jacques Revel, *Jeux d'echelles: La micro-analyse à l'expérience*, ed. Jacques Revel (Paris: Gallimard Le Seuil, 1996); Jan de Vries, 'Playing with Scales: The Global and the Micro, the Macro and the Nano', *Past & Present* 242, no. 14 (2019): 23–36.

42 See, for instance, Jan Rüger, 'OXO: Or, the Challenges of Transnational History', *European History Quarterly* 40, no. 4 (January 2010): 656–68; Ángel Alcalde, 'Spatializing Transnational History: European Spaces and Territories', *European Review of History / Revue Européenne d'Histoire* 25, nos. 3–4 (July 2018): 553–67.

Chapter 1

Grassroots internationalism from small places: pen, ink and the forging of friendships in a constructed language

On 26 June 1908, a postcard was sent from Harmanli, Bulgaria, to 'Sro Rev. J. Beveridge, 8 Prospect Place, Dundee, Skotlando'. The image illustrating the front of the postcard is split into two. The upper half displays a photographic image of Harmanli, showing a small-town setting with a number of family homes, one or two larger buildings and what appears to be a mosque in the background. The title of the postcard – in both Bulgarian, using the Cyrillic script, and in French, using the Latin script[1] – reads: 'View from the city of Harmanli'. The bottom half shows a photo of a stone bridge reaching over a calm and shallow river. For the occasion of the photo, a group of some twenty townspeople are lined up on top of the bridge while a few others – and a dog – stand below it on the bank of the river lined by trees. All face the camera.

As a communication technology, postcards emerged around 1870 and soon became standardised in size and format – typically with one of their sides divided, with a middle line separating the address from the written content. The text and photographic images became increasingly popular after the 1890s.[2] Dundee, John Beveridge's hometown, soon became a centre of postcard production during this boom.[3] While postcards were no longer a novelty in 1908, when this postcard from rural Bulgaria reached the Beveridge household, John Beveridge may have felt a sense of excitement.

Figure 1.1: Postcard sent from Harmanli, Bulgaria, to John Beveridge, 1908. The photograph shows the town of Harmanli, Bulgaria, and the Maritsa River, c. 1908. Source: John Beveridge Collection, Ms36242/114. Courtesy of the University of St Andrews Libraries and Museums, ID: ms36242-ms36244

In 1908, that postcard may have offered him his only glimpse of such a faraway and unfamiliar place like Harmanli.

Postcards are rather ephemeral objects. A few words quickly jotted down, sent, received, read and, at some point, likely thrown away. The card from Harmanli arrived in Dundee during the 'golden age' of the postcard, the period between 1895 and 1915 when paper objects became a mass phenomenon. During these years, around 200–300 billion postcards were produced worldwide. In Britain alone, around one billion postcards were dispatched in 1906; postmen made several deliveries a day in urban areas.[4] Unlike books, postcards tend to have a short-lived lifespan and purpose. Yet they zigzagged across Europe and played a vital role in the emergence and shaping of the Esperanto community.[5]

Contrasting with the bulk of the historiography on Esperanto and constructed languages, it is the desk of John Beveridge at 8 Prospect Place in Dundee that takes centre stage here, not Zamenhof's desk in Warsaw. Starting from a close reading of a selection of postcards mailed to Dundee around 1910, this chapter outlines how postcards, postal stamps, yearbooks, address lists and periodicals give us clues to understand the emergence of local and regional Esperanto clusters in small towns and semi-rural places in Scotland, Bulgaria, Finland and elsewhere.

Esperantujo – the language community, where *-uj-* is the suffix denoting a container – allows for a decentring of European history through a transnational perspective.[6] Designed for international communication, Esperanto realises its full potential through border-crossing exchanges, which partly explains the geographical dispersion of this language community. With Esperanto speakers present potentially everywhere but concentrated nowhere,[7] the language offers a vantage point from which we can overcome an approach focusing on centres and margins by considering how ordinary language users such as John Beveridge constitute a node within Esperantujo – where people connected with one another between thousands of places, small and big, dotted across Europe and beyond.

The notion of decentralisation is key here. With the lens zoomed in on Dundee and Beveridge, we can recast the history of international communication from the perspective of an ordinary member of the first generation of Esperanto speakers and showcase the routine with which people like him made use of the language at the turn of the century. Through a grassroots form of internationalism, John Beveridge, along with thousands of other Esperanto speakers, practised foreign languages, exchanged postal stamps and discussed topics such as architecture, religion and world affairs. As mundane as these exchanges may appear, they illustrate a form of curiosity and worldliness that connected distant places and individuals who never met face to face.

Such practices of grassroots internationalism mediated by correspondence rarely feature in scholarship on institutionalised internationalism – which, in turn, is epitomised by world congresses, international bodies, expert communities, the labour movement or women's organisations.[8] However, they matter in understanding how ordinary people effectively engaged with globalisation beyond commonplace images of steamships, aeroplanes and the Universal Exhibitions associated with *La Belle Époque*, which were out of reach for most people at the turn of the century.

The bridge between Scotland and Bulgaria

As a fragile link between Scotland and a rural place in wider Esperantujo, the postcard from Harmanli was only one of over fifty that John Beveridge received between 1908 and 1910.[9] While a few more pieces of correspondence were certainly sent back and forth, this postcard is one of the few surviving sources that allow us to reconstruct this connection between Dundee and Harmanli.

The postcards sent to John Beveridge point to an uneven archival situation. We know much more about Beveridge than about his correspondents. We know which correspondents wrote to Beveridge but, in most cases, we do not know what he wrote or whether he responded at all. We can safely assume that most of Beveridge's correspondents were ordinary Esperanto speakers, who could be members of local Esperanto clubs and who might or might not have used the language to participate in international Esperanto congresses and meet fellow speakers in person.

In many ways, John Beveridge was also an ordinary Esperanto speaker. As a Presbyterian clergyman, he looked after his parish and lived with his family of six, among them his four children. In his free time, he took to Esperanto to communicate and correspond with people outside Dundee about various topics of his interest. He was, after all, an active member of the Dundee Esperanto Club (which we discuss in detail in Chapter 2), served as the first President of the Scottish Esperanto Federation in 1909–10, and travelled abroad to participate in the 1912 Universal Congress of Esperanto in Kraków – the only one he ever attended.

The trip to Kraków may have been the pinnacle of John Beveridge's life with Esperanto. For a few days in the summer of 1912, he met fellow Esperanto speakers from across the world. Yet, John Beveridge's overall engagement with the language was not one of mobility. For him and his correspondents, Esperanto was primarily a venture that involved writing, sending and receiving postcards and letters, and participating in a community of strangers connected by emerging technologies. Esperanto and postcards were two of these and a perfect match.

In the communicative landscape around 1900, with novel technologies ranging from telegraphy and telephony to photography, the image of Harmanli may have been the only glimpse of a rural Bulgarian town John Beveridge would ever acquire, as well as the most direct link to the person Beveridge corresponded with. Gathering for the photo on the Harmanli postcard in Figure 1.1, the men by the bridge may have looked familiar and yet different to what Beveridge witnessed in his everyday life. Some are wearing beards and hats, some are smoking pipes, as was the custom in those days. Some men may have been local townspeople, craftsmen or landowners. Three men are wearing some kind of uniform, as they perhaps were local gendarmes, officers or military personnel. Also, a few fellow clergymen appear in the picture. Yet this is where things may have looked less familiar to Beveridge, as they are donned in a dark cloak and hat, both reminiscent of the eastern Orthodox church. Two men on the bank of the river, one sitting and one with a dog on a leash, appear to be wearing a turban and Muslim attire.

Bulgaria was only nine years older than Esperanto. A territory of the Ottoman Empire for several hundred years, Bulgaria became a principality in 1878. Its boundaries were contested, leading to numerous treaties and warfare between Bulgaria and Serbia before the former effectively became an independent state in September 1908. Smaller than and different from the initial 1878 boundaries, the new state had a sizeable Muslim community.[10]

We may not know how much John Beveridge knew about Bulgaria, but the postcard provided him with at least a snapshot of this distant place. The piece of correspondence from Harmanli was sent in June 1908, just months before the country at the other end of Europe declared independence. So, what was the content of the postcard once Beveridge turned from the image side to the written text? His correspondent wrote the following (Figure 1.2):

> Estimata samideano,[11] Kun tiu ĉi letero mi sciigas vin ke mi ricevis la markojn kiun vi sendas al mia frato St. Kirilov kiu estas forveturinta alian urbon kie li restos 2 monatoj kaj kredu kiam estos reveninta tuje respondas al vi. Mi petas bonvole respondi por la ricevo de mia karto.
>
> Kun saluto samideana
>
> Fina Nedenka Kirilova Harmanli Bulgarujo.[12]

As short as the text is, this exchange offers several clues that substantiate key aspects of the then emerging Esperanto community.[13] First, the sender was only partially familiar with Esperanto, which becomes evident in the language errors in the brief message and the lack of any indication of a sophisticated command of the language. Second, assuming that her first language was Bulgarian, she was likely more used to Cyrillic and, for this reason, perhaps not accustomed to writing in the Latin script. Hence, just as with the bridge in the image, writing in Esperanto denoted here an attempt to leave one's linguistic comfort zone to build bridges between

Figure 1.2: Postcard sent from Harmanli, Bulgaria, to John Beveridge, 1908. John Beveridge Collection, Ms36242/114. Courtesy of the University of St Andrews Libraries and Museums, ID: ms36242-ms36244

people from different linguistic backgrounds – in this case, a bridge connecting a Bulgarian speaker and an English speaker.

Additionally, the content was about a rather mundane form of internationalism: the interest in and exchange of stamps. This was in fact not uncommon among Esperanto speakers, given how stamp collecting and philately were fashionable at the time.[14] Around 1900, it must have been exciting to receive stamps from an out-of-the-way place that would otherwise remain unknown. As mundane as this exchange between Dundee and Harmanli may seem, it points towards another common thread in the use of Esperanto: an openness and curiosity about the world and other peoples.[15]

Finally, the sender signs off as 'Nedenka Kirilova', as someone responding on behalf of 'my brother St. Kirilov'. The person John Beveridge initially contacted and sent postal stamps to must have been a man named Stoičo

Kirilov – and Nedenka Kirilova, his sister. How did these three people find one another?

Yearbooks, address directories and postal stamps: mapping Esperantujo through its exchanges

One way for Esperanto speakers to locate potential pen pals was through the *Jarlibro* – the yearbook that listed the addresses of fellow speakers around the world. Beyond the act of designing a language, the making of Esperantujo also involved gathering people who were willing to learn and use Esperanto. In this regard, the *Jarlibro* became one of the backbones of what would progressively develop as a networked and interconnected language community.

When Ludwik Zamenhof published the first Esperanto textbook – later known as *Unua Libro* (First Book, 1887) – he included a postcard-like coupon on the final page of this booklet. This detachable coupon was an invitation for readers interested in the language to send their contact details back to Zamenhof, so that he could compile a directory containing the names and contact details of those committed to learning Esperanto.[16]

It did not take long for these coupons to reach Warsaw. From 1889 to 1908, the names and addresses of Esperanto speakers were published in the *Adresaro de la personoj, kiuj ellernis la lingvon 'Esperanto'* (Directory of the Persons Who Learned the Language 'Esperanto').[17] From 1904, these address lists were regularly published by the Paris-based publishing house Hachette as *Tutmonda Jarlibro Esperantista* (Worldwide Esperantist Yearbook). Each volume consisted of over 300 pages with an ever-growing list of Esperanto speakers and clubs catalogued by country.

While the people listed in these yearbooks and address directories were mostly strangers to each other and lived in different – usually geographically disconnected – places, these directories allowed any person anywhere to reach out to fellow Esperanto speakers. Zamenhof did not expect them to know one another or ever meet one another in person – although many did at the level of international Esperanto congresses. Rather, the *Jarlibro* aimed to enable those who were willing and curious to forge distant friendships and communicate with pen pals. Congresses – in particular the annual international congresses held from 1905 onwards – were certainly a highlight of the Esperanto experience, but only for those who had the time and financial means to attend them. On a daily basis, however, the making of

Esperantujo relied not on large gatherings but on the ability to find one another and maintain contact through the postal system. Esperanto had not just been devised as a bridge of words between language communities: it became a bridge between places.[18]

John Beveridge owned two editions of the *Jarlibro*, from 1907 and 1910. As a member of the Dundee Esperanto Club, he participated in social gatherings at the local level, yet the major purpose and excitement of Esperanto was to reach beyond the local. A key way to do so was via correspondence.

Back to the Harmanli postcard, the 1907 *Jarlibro* lists an Esperanto group by the name of 'Progreso' (Progress) in Harmanli.[19] The club was founded in November 1906, around two years after the Dundee club. Both clubs were part of a wider boom, in particular in 1905 and 1906, as the first international congress of Esperanto in 1905 had given the emerging community a boost and as newspapers across Europe were covering Esperanto extensively.[20] But what did Esperanto in Bulgaria look like?

In 1907, the Harmanli group consisted of thirteen members – eleven men and two women – including the president, a certain Velev Jurdan and the secretary, Stoičo Kirilov. This was the man John Beveridge reached out to (or back) in order to exchange stamps. While Stoičo Kirilov is elusive, Velev Jurdan is listed in the *Jarlibro* as a shoemaker, and four other club members were merchants. The two women were unmarried and described as 'fraŭlino' (Miss). Nedenka Kirilova is not listed as a member of the local club, yet she had at least a basic command of the language. Therefore, however systematic the *Jarlibro* might have been to map this non-territorial community, it did not capture all Esperanto learners and speakers.

Centring this analysis on a postcard from Harmanli may seem unusual but, as a place, Harmanli is interesting in itself. Small, unassuming and relatively unknown, the town is located about halfway along a trade route between Sofia and Istanbul. Harmanli was then multilingual, situated in an imperial borderland in flux with Bulgarian and Turkish speakers not far from the soon-to-be Bulgarian state borders, with Greece to the south. If Dundee was enmeshed in the jute and whaling trade, Harmanli was entangled in the trade of territories and the conflicts that went with it. Both were, in different ways, small but nonetheless geopolitically significant.

Harmanli and, more broadly, Bulgaria may not be the first places one has in mind when thinking about Esperanto or about a transnational history of Europe. However, they constitute intriguingly active clusters in early Esperanto history. After the very first Esperanto clubs emerged in Nürnberg (1888), Uppsala (1891), St Petersburg (1892) and Odessa (1894), a club was founded in Plovdiv, Bulgaria, in 1901, along with a Bulgara Societo Esperantista. Three years later, we find Esperanto speakers and clubs in 114 places across Bulgaria, a rather astonishing number for a relatively small country.[21]

Some clubs like the one in Plovdiv featured 51 members by 1904. Silistra, located on the border with Romania, had 88 members, while the *Jarlibro* lists 106 Esperanto speakers in Sofia. These were the larger cities, and in a city like Sofia the dominant professions among the local Esperanto speakers were *oficisto* (white-collar worker or civil servant), *soldato* (military personnel), *instruisto* (teacher) and *studento* (student). In Plovdiv, a fair number of Esperanto speakers were listed as *telefonisto* (telephone operator), *stenografisto* (stenographer) and *telegrafisto* (telegrapher). These were people that dealt on a daily basis with the latest communication technologies in their professional lives. Many others, in places like Pleven or Harmanli, appear as *komercisto* (merchant). For professionals like merchants and telephone operators, Esperanto had a practical and functional element. It was appealing to learn a language that allowed for easy and effective cross-border communication, at a time when *Bulgara Esperantisto* – one of the at least five Esperanto periodicals existing in Bulgaria around 1900 – regularly listed a number of Bulgarians who 'deziras interŝangi ilustritajn poŝtkartojn, gazetojn kaj markojn' (wish to exchange illustrated postcards, magazines and postal stamps).[22]

The striking pattern, however, lies beyond the larger cities and beyond the political, commercial and cultural hubs. Out of the overall 114 places where Esperanto speakers are listed in Bulgaria in 1904, a total of 61 places only had one or two speakers, and another 15 places only had three speakers at the time. Even though many of these people were in semi-rural areas and villages, they were part of the interconnected world of Esperantujo, most likely simply yearning to learn about the world beyond a small town in Bulgaria.[23] However surprising, the distribution of Esperanto speakers in Bulgaria was consequential: Bulgaria was a nation-state in the making at the time.[24] In it, amidst Greek, Turkish and Romanian speakers, Esperanto fell on fertile ground. It became associated with a certain vision of modernity – one rooted in a quest for mutual understanding through an international auxiliary language thought of as a means to overcome language barriers and nationalist rivalries.

Figure 1.3: Postcard sent from Kymi, Finland, to John Beveridge, 1910. The photograph shows Hugo Salokannel. Source: John Beveridge Collection, Ms364242/116. Courtesy of the University of St Andrews Libraries and Museums, ID: ms36242-ms36244

Greetings from Kymi: a railway station in Finland and its vegetarian officer

The postcard from Harmanli was not unique. John Beveridge corresponded with many other Esperanto speakers on a range of topics, including the mutual exchange of stamps and other shared interests. Postcards from Turku and Kymi in Finland, from Hradec Králové in Austria–Hungary or from Sarajevo in Bosnia arrived in 1908 alongside stamps and further addresses of potential Esperanto pen pals.

One such postcard was sent to Dundee from Kymi in August 1908 by John Beveridge's pen pal Hugo Salokannel (1880–1966). This was one of at least three mails Beveridge received from Salokannel between 1908 and 1910, which indicates a more sustained correspondence. In this postcard, Salokannel thanked Beveridge for his previous postcard, also sending the latter a photograph of the former: 'La kostumo, en kiu mi estas vestita reprezentas tiun de fervojistoj en Finnlando' (The outfit in which I am dressed represents that of the railway workers in Finland). In return, Salokannel asked Beveridge to send a photo of himself so that he could add it to his album, ending his postcard with 'Amikan saluton!' (Friendly salutations!). The correspondence between the two had sparked a personal interest in seeing the face and attire of the person at the other end of the exchange, pointing to their curiosity to get to know one another within Esperantujo.

Beside his photo, Salokannel listed the addresses of three Finnish Esperanto speakers, recommending Beveridge to contact them to further exchange postcards and stamps. The three locations – in the towns of Kymi, Karhula and Hyvinkää – were, respectively, in rural southern Finland, north of Helsinki and further east on the southern coast. These locations epitomised geographical patterns akin to the previously described Harmanli and the wider small-town Esperanto landscape in Bulgaria.

Browsing through the *Jarlibro*, none of these locations seemed to have a local club. Kymi only had one Esperanto speaker in 1904 – another railway officer, by the name Wilhelm Lönnqvist.[25] Tampere and Helsinki hosted the only two Esperanto clubs listed in Finland at the time. While Bulgaria boasted many more clubs and had overall far more locations with a few Esperanto speakers than Finland, paying attention to these two countries illustrates a striking pattern: Esperanto had reached the rural hinterlands of Europe. If we imagine the world around 1908 from small-town settings like Kymi or Harmanli, the possibility of getting a glimpse of distant places via postcards, stamps or a photograph featuring a person's face and outfit must have been thrilling. These exchanges gave pen pals a sense of participation in a much wider world than everyday life in a small town otherwise allowed.[26]

It is important to consider that Esperanto did not just come to these people, nor was it imposed on them by a hegemonic nation-state or by Zamenhof. People like Beveridge, Kirilov and Salokannel actively reached out for Esperanto, and they embraced it on their own terms. Technologies and infrastructure from railways and telegraphy to a well-oiled, cross-border postal system had reached these places then, making them more connected than they were a few decades earlier.[27] Esperanto, then, emerged as an ideal tool that, aligned with these novel technologies, allowed ordinary people to partake in this wave of globalisation. In many ways, beyond being a language, Esperanto was just another invention of the time.

Revealing in terms of the popularity of forging friendships across Esperantujo are the closing lines of Hugo Salokannel's earlier-mentioned postcard: 'Ĉu vi havas multajn korespondantojn? Mi havas ilin nun tro multe' (Do you have many correspondents? I now have too many of them). By his own account, Salokannel, the railway station officer stationed near Karhula, some eighty kilometres east of Helsinki, was heavily invested in Esperanto correspondence networks by 1908.

As rural and unassuming as his life may have been, Salokannel lived a very active life for an Esperanto speaker. He learned Esperanto around 1904, becoming proficient in it a few years later.[28] The postcard itself demonstrates elegance, sophistication and familiarity with writing in the language. Both Beveridge and Salokannel were first-generation Esperanto speakers, yet they crossed paths with Esperanto at different stages of their lives: Beveridge was in his early to mid-forties, while Salokannel was in his early twenties. Born in 1880, Hugo Salokannel was indeed of the same generation as John Beveridge's daughters. Esperanto, it seems, did not just bridge distance and first languages but also generations. Despite their age difference, the twenty-something-year-old Finnish railway officer and the middle-aged Scottish clergyman had much in common, after all.

Both served as presidents of their respective national Esperanto associations – that is, the Finnish Esperanto Association and the Scottish Esperanto Federation. Both shared an interest in religion: Salokannel was the editor of the periodical *Kristana Espero* (Christian Hope), whereas Beveridge was involved in the translation of the New Testament.[29] Nonetheless, there were differences that may point to their respective ages at the time of writing and what they did with the language. Salokannel, it seems, was far more of an activist. He embraced several values, such as pacifism and vegetarianism, that resonated with fellow Esperanto speakers of his generation.[30] Such reformist ideals and alternative lifestyles indeed overlapped with the internationalist ideals linked to Esperanto. The decades around 1900 were after all a time of rapid transformation, with the heyday of empires, consumerism and industrialisation in Europe and beyond. Yet it was also a moment of counter movements and cultures, as well as various forms of resistance, from anarchism to terrorism as well as vegetarianism.[31]

Between 1914 and late in his life in the 1950s, Hugo Salokannel published in both Esperanto and Finnish, occasionally under the penname Bontemplano – Good Templar, perhaps indicating his connection with Christianity. Among his works were reflections on Christianity, Esperanto learning materials and song collections, as well as a short autobiography.[32] Looking at the two pen pals, it seems that the younger one embraced a more idealistic version of what Esperanto offered.[33] Moreover, as a young railway officer, Salokannel was perhaps among the vanguard of workers – railway workers in particular – that flocked to Esperanto in the first half of the twentieth century.

Figure 1.4: Postcard sent from Kymi, Finland to John Beveridge, 1910. The photograph shows a group of Esperanto speakers on a boat on the Gulf of Finland, 1910. John Beveridge Collection, Ms36242/172. Courtesy of the University of St Andrews Libraries and Museums, ID: ms36242-ms36244

A further postcard by Hugo Salokannel displays a photograph of a group of twenty-seven people on a boat, with a short note explaining that these were members of the Esperanto groups of Kymi and Kotka in an outing on the Finnish Gulf in late May 1910. Salokannel marked himself with an 'X', but Beveridge may have identified him anyway given the earlier photograph sent to the latter.

As popular as mass-produced postcards were, this one must have been a personalised, commissioned one. It is safe to assume that more than one copy of this postcard was produced and others may have been sent out into Esperantujo. In addition to the thousands of names listed in the *Jarlibro*, the faces and the people in the photograph give rare hints about the social composition of local Esperanto clubs in Finland at the time.

The group of Finnish Esperanto speakers depicted here illustrates the attraction and social appeal the language had. It shows teenagers – if not children – folks in their twenties and middle-aged women and men, some wearing distinctly middle-class outfits and hats. People were surely dressed for the day trip, most of them with clothing resembling Hugo Salokannel's. They may have been colleagues from the railway or from other professions along the lower middle-classes. In other words, they were local, ordinary folks. Yet they were members of the Esperanto groups in Kymi and Kotka, and as such, provincial rank-and-file Esperanto speakers.

We may never know the names behind their faces, who these people were, what professions they had or what kind of lives they lived. Yet it is fair to assume that their reasons for learning an international auxiliary language did not end here on a boat on the Gulf of Finland. These people surely had similar aspirations and interests to Salokannel's and Beveridge's. They likely read the periodical *Finna Esperantisto* and had access to Esperanto magazines from abroad as these were sent back and forth between groups and members, and some of them may have had pen pals abroad.

The correspondence between John Beveridge and Hugo Salokannel lasted for at least two years. The latest recorded postcard from Salokannel to Beveridge was sent on 20 July 1910. In a brief message, the Finnish railway officer thanked Beveridge for 'via bona kaj bela verketo' (your good and beautiful booklet) and concluded with 'Estu honoro al Dio!' (May God be honoured!). Even though the number of mails exchanged between them is unclear, the content of the three surviving postcards points to a sustained correspondence, and their friendship clearly evolved beyond the exchange of postal stamps. The sheer brevity of Salokannel's messages suggests a certain familiarity and routine-like correspondence between the two, ranging from thanks and acknowledgements of receipt to insights into life in rural Finland.

Postcards and pen pals: the making of friendships and of Esperantujo

Frequent requests for postal stamps reveal one of the systematic approaches John Beveridge used to build his network of correspondents. Like many other Esperanto speakers, Beveridge likely placed a note of interest in exchanging postcards and stamps in *The British Esperantist* or another periodical, which fellow Esperanto speakers then responded to. This communication system – based on yearbooks, address directories and periodicals – was widely used: magazines like *Ruslanda Esperantisto* (Russian Esperantist) or *Fervoja Esperantisto* (Railway Esperantist), to name just a few, regularly printed lists of names or personal adverts from individuals seeking postal exchanges.[34] Just as Salokannel had 'too many' pen pals, other Esperanto speakers took pride in their extensive collections of stamps from several countries. Remarks on one's pen pals and stamp collections demonstrate the enthusiasm of Esperanto speakers for developing their worldliness.

As some of the postcards above illustrate, John Beveridge's exchanges with his correspondents frequently went beyond icebreakers and postal stamps. In return for some stamps, Leo Jalava, a correspondent from Turku, sent Beveridge a copy of the periodical *Finna Esperantisto*.[35] Jalava pointed his Dundee pen pal to the translation of *Shylock* in this edition. The poem by Swedish poet Oscar Levertin (1862–1906) had been translated by Hjalmar Johannes Runeberg (1874–1934). The latter, as Jalava explained, was among 'la plej favoraj esperantistoj finnaj' (one of the most auspicious Finnish Esperanto speakers). Runeberg – whose photograph featured on the front side of that postcard – was indeed one of the Esperanto pioneers in Finland: Runeberg learned the language in Paris in 1901, attended the very first international congress of Esperanto, translated Swedish and Danish literature into the language and, ultimately, became the first president of the Finnish Esperanto Association.[36] Through exchanging periodicals, poems and translations of religious works and literature, these pen pals learned about each other's personal pursuits, discussed their mutual interests and engendered meaningful social connections, intellectual links and friendship.[37]

John Beveridge received many more mail items along similar lines and partly as a response to his notes of interest published in Esperanto periodicals. Alongside postcards, he received magazines including *Amerika Esperantisto* (US), various editions of *Brazilia Revuo Esperantista* (Brazil), *La Verda Standardo* (Hungary) and *La Suno Hispana* (Spain) in 1907–8.[38] Similarly, a certain Feliks Knapski – a merchant and member of the Esperanto club in Łódź – thanked John Beveridge for sending him English-Esperanto learning materials and, in return, Knapski sent an edition of *Pola Esperantisto* (Poland).[39] Lastly, in 1910, correspondents from Superaguy (Brazil), Tiflis (Georgia) and Madras (India/British Empire) thanked Beveridge for mailing them the booklet *Prediko sur la Monto*, Beveridge's translation of the *Sermon on the Mount*.[40] In particular, Beveridge's interests in Nordic cultures and languages, as well as theology, seemed to have contributed to distant yet close correspondent friendships that spanned continents.

Another common thread that brings together many of Beveridge's pieces of correspondence relates to an attention to architectural styles of the world. Architecture, then, illustrates what we hinted at above regarding the worldliness and curiosity about other peoples that many Esperanto speakers shared. Pen pals from Hradec Králové, Nový Bydžov and Sarajevo (Austria–Hungary), as well as from Flöha (German Empire),[41] featured sights or architectural landmarks ranging from churches, hotels and historical sites to wide boulevards. One correspondent from Göteborg (Sweden) thanked John Beveridge for sending an image of Dundee's Wishart Arch and, in return, sent a postcard featuring King's Gate Avenue, 'unu de niaj plej belaj stratoj' (one of our most beautiful streets). The Swedish pen pal added that Göteborg had been built during the reign of Gustav Adolf by Dutch architects and thus shared many features with cities like Antwerp.[42]

Another correspondent, a certain Francisko Sladý, sent greetings from Kutná Hora (Austria–Hungary) in 1908. Sladý explained the architectural site featured on the postcard as being part of the Italian court and former seat of Bohemian monarchs.[43] The two postcards sent from Hradec Králové and Nový Bydžov (also in Bohemia, Austria–Hungary) were signed with the correspondents' names and occupations – respectively a *komercisto* (merchant) and a *studento* (student). None of these correspondents appear in the many versions of the *Jarlibro* or in lists of participants of the Universal Congresses of Esperanto in those years. Yet it does not come as a surprise that Bohemia featured on John Beveridge's map of Esperantujo so prominently. From Prague to southern and eastern Bohemia, the Esperanto landscape was booming at the time, with big cities and small towns like Pardubice, Kutná Hora and Kukleny also hosting Esperanto clubs specifically oriented to women and to workers.[44]

Concluding remarks

In the early decades of the twentieth century, businesspeople, merchants, government representatives and intellectuals experienced internationalism through trips, international congresses and cross-border interactions of all sorts in other languages, without resorting to Esperanto. However, these opportunities were not available to most people, such as those Esperanto speakers who sent correspondence to Scotland from Bulgaria, Finland, Brazil or Austria–Hungary. After all, most of John Beveridge's interlocutors were simply students, civil servants and railway workers, who had no financial means or professional opportunities to experience such heightened forms of internationalism.

For them, correspondence exchange in Esperanto with their pen pals abroad offered a simple yet feasible and surely exciting way of connecting with the wider world. Through this form of language-based, grassroots internationalism mediated by correspondence, these ordinary people encountered fellows with whom they not only shared a language, but who were also curious about their interlocutors and eager to keep the conversation going. And this brings us to a discussion about scales.

One could describe Geneva – the city that housed the headquarters of the Universala Esperanto-Asocio (World Esperanto Association, UEA) between 1908 and 1936 – or Dresden – where some 1,200 Esperanto speakers came together for the Fourth Universal Congress of Esperanto in 1908[45] – as the capital cities or centres of the Esperanto community. Regardless of how one may define the key geographies constituting this dispersed community, John Beveridge's Dundee certainly would not feature on such a list in 1908. Hence, our experiment of placing John Beveridge's postcards at the core of our narrative reveals unexpected layers of Esperantujo – of a language community that is (and relies on being) geographically dispersed and multisited in its own right.[46] After all, without the multilingualism and internationalism that such dispersion afforded, the use of an international auxiliary language would not reach its full potential.

Beginning our analysis from Dundee has brought us to places like Harmanli, Kymi and Kutná Hora. Yet, why would someone from these relatively 'marginal' places learn and use Esperanto? Perhaps this is precisely what made Esperanto and these friendships so significant to these people: the fact that Esperanto and correspondence provided them with an entryway to a set of grassroots internationalist experiences they might not have had otherwise. In Geneva, Dresden, Paris or Prague, the plethora of Esperanto courses and clubs available gave people plenty of opportunities to join this community. In small places hosting only one or two Esperanto speakers, in turn, Esperanto lived up to the promise of forging distant, yet meaningful connections across linguistic and geographical boundaries.

Despite the seemingly small size of some of these villages and towns, it would be incorrect to categorise them as marginal, peripheral or isolated. On the contrary, the postcards analysed here reveal how some of the ordinary people living in these places were well connected. These people and places were presumably on the fringes of technological developments, modernity and globalisation at the turn of the century, at a time when units of measurement were being standardised, literacy rates were increasing and postal services were progressively becoming more affordable to the lower middle classes. This marginality was not the case, however, as people in these places also partook in the transnational exchanges that postal services and an international auxiliary language could afford – which, ultimately, collapses the dichotomy of centre versus peripheries/margins.

Individuals like Beveridge, Kirilov, Salokannel and Jalava epitomise how Esperanto provided an effective communicative tool to complement the wider technological developments of the time. However simple, postcards in Esperanto conveyed a hint of what the skyline of a Bulgarian city looked like and what kinds of clothes railway workers donned in Finland. In exchanging postal stamps, these grassroots internationalists also learned about the habits and poems of other countries, discovered the shapes and historical backgrounds of architectural styles from abroad, saw each other's faces and attires – and, in the process, made friends. This is perhaps where the main trait of *samideanoj* (fellow thinkers, as Esperanto speakers frequently refer to each other) lies. Ultimately, more than a matter of being able to communicate, it is a matter of being interested and deeply invested in communicating, with the language itself working as a mechanism to bring people together on the basis of this effort towards worldliness.

Notes

1 French was then used as the language of international postal services, see F. H. Williamson, 'The International Postal Service and the Universal Postal Union', *Journal of the Royal Institute of International Affairs*, 9, no. 1 (1930), 68–78.

2 Julia Gillen and Nigel Hall, 'Edwardian Postcards: Illuminating Ordinary Writing', in *The Anthropology of Writing: Understanding Textually Mediated Worlds*, ed. David Barton and Uta Papen (London: Bloomsbury, 2012), 169–89.

3 Kevin J. James, Melissa McAfee, Aritra Bhattacharjee, Alexandra Kurceba and Ainsley Robertson, 'Greetings from Scotland: Postcards and the Digitisation of Travel Ephemera in the University of Guelph's Scottish Collections', *The International Review of Scottish Studies*, 44 (2019), 3–9.

4 Bjarne Rogan, 'An Entangled Object: The Picture Postcard as Souvenir and Collectible, Exchange and Ritual Communication', *Cultural Analysis* 4 (2005): 1–27; Yehiel Limor and Ilan Tamir, 'The Neglected Medium: Postage Stamps as Mass Media', *Communication Theory* 31, no. 3 (2021): 491–505; Ana Fumurescu, *Visualizing Agency: Postcards and Romanian National Identity* (Bloomington, IN: Indiana University Press, 2015).

5 See Konstantinos Andriotis and Mišela Mavrič, 'Postcard Mobility: Going Beyond Image and Text', *Annals of Tourism Research* 40, no. 1 (2013): 18–39; David Prochaska and Jordana Mendelson, eds, *Postcards: Ephemeral Histories of Modernity* (University Park: Pennsylvania State University Press, 2010).

6 Natalie Zemon Davis, 'Decentering History: Local Stories and Cultural Crossings in a Global World', *History and Theory* 50, no. 2 (2011): 188–202, here 190; Pierre-Yves Saunier, *Transnational History (Basingstoke: Palgrave Macmillan, 2013)*; Clavin, 'Defining Transnationalism', *Contemporary European History* 14, no. 4 (2005): 421–39, here 438; Struck et al. 'Introduction', 577.

7 Richard Wood, 'A Voluntary Non-Ethnic, Non-Territorial Speech Community', in *Sociolinguistic Studies in Language Contact: Methods and Cases*, ed. William Francis Mackey and Jacob Ornstein (The Hague: Mouton, 1979), 433–50.

8 See, for instance, Glenda Sluga, *Internationalism in the Age of Nationalism* (Philadelphia: University of Pennsylvania Press, 2013); Davide Rodogno, Bernhard Struck and Jakob Vogel, eds, *Shaping the Transnational Sphere: Experts, Networks and Issues from the 1840s to the 1930s* (New York: Berghahn, 2014); David Brydan and Jessica Reinisch, eds, *Internationalists in European History: Rethinking the Twentieth Century* (London: Bloomsbury Academic, 2021); Jessica Reinisch, 'Introduction: Agents of Internationalism', *Contemporary European History* 25, no. 2 (2016): 195–205; Leila J. Rupp, 'Constructing Internationalism: The Case of Transnational Women's Organizations, 1888–1945', *The American Historical Review* 99, no. 5 (1994): 1571–600; Glenda Sluga and Patricia Clavin, eds, *Internationalisms: A Twentieth-Century History* (Cambridge: Cambridge University Press, 2016).

9 John Beveridge Collection, Ms36242/198.

10 See Mary Neuburger, *The Orient Within: Muslim Minorities and the Negotiation of Nationhood in Modern Bulgaria* (Ithaca, NY: Cornell University Press, 2011), 19–23; Emily Greble, *Muslims and the Making of Modern Europe* (Oxford: Oxford University Press, 2021), 25; John Connelly, *From Peoples into Nations: A History of Eastern Europe* (Princeton: Princeton University Press, 2020), 217–18, 229–30.

11 The literal translation of *samideano* into English is 'fellow thinker'. Commonly used as a self-referential term among Esperanto speakers, *samideano* draws on the assumption that Esperanto speakers would share not only the language but also a set of internationalist ideals. See Fians, *Esperanto Revolutionaries and Geeks*, 105–6; Forster, *The Esperanto Movement*, 82.

12 'Dear fellow thinker, with this letter I inform you that I have received the stamps that you send to my brother St. Kirilov who is about to travel to another city where he will be staying for 2 months and believe me when he returns he will immediately reply to you. Please reply to the receipt of my card. With regards, fellow thinker Miss Nedenka Kirilova Harmanli Bulgaria'.

13 See Matti Peltonen, 'Clues, Margins, and Monads: The Micro-Macro Link in Historical Research', *History and Theory*, 40, no. 3 (2001): 347–59.

14 See Limor and Tamir, 'The Neglected Medium', 491–505; Steven Gelber, 'Free Market Metaphor: The Historical Dynamics of Stamp Collecting', *Comparative Studies in Society and History* 4, no. 34 (1992): 742–69.

15 O'Keeffe, *Esperanto and Languages of Internationalism*, 74; Guilherme Fians, 'La Kosmopolito kaj la Aliulo: Historiaj konsideroj pri diferenco kaj diverseco laŭ la vidpunkto de esperantistoj', in *En la Mondon Venis Nova Lingvo: Festlibro por la 75-Jariĝo de Ulrich Lins*, ed. Hitosi Gotoo, Goro Christoph Kimura and José Antonio Vergara (New York: Mondial, 2018), 475–95.

16 Forster, *The Esperanto Movement*, 55.

17 The first volume was Ludwik Lejzer Zamenhof, *Adresaro de la personoj, kiuj ellernis la lingvon 'Esperanto'* (Warsaw: Zamenhof, 1889). See Garvía, *Esperanto and Its Rivals*, 95, 183.

18 For a brief account on Esperanto pen pals who exchanged postcards within the Soviet Union, see O'Keeffe, *Esperanto and Languages of Internationalism*, 73–7.

19 Ménil, Félicien de, ed., *Tutmonda Jarlibro Esperantista Enhavanta La Adresaron de Dro Zamenhof por 1907* (Paris: Hachette, 1907), 167.

20 See, for instance, 'The Language of the Future: The Development of Esperanto', *The Daily News*, September 22, 1905; 'Esperanto', *The Times*, August 12, 1905; 'The Boulogne Esperanto Congress', *The Times*, August 11, 1905; 'Progress of Esperanto', *Evening Standard*, August 11, 1905; 'Esperanto Weltkongress', *Allgemeine Zeitung*, February 5, 1908; 'Le Congrès universel espérantiste', *Le Progrès*, September, 1906.

21 Ménil, Félicien de, ed., *Tutmonda Jarlibro Esperantista Enhavanta La Adresaron de Dro Zamenhof por 1904* (Paris: Hachette, 1904), x, 55–63. See also Forster, *The Esperanto Movement,* 19–20; on early Esperanto clubs, see Garvía, *Esperanto and Its Rivals*, 45–7.

22 *Bulgara Esperantisto*, March, 1907, 10.

23 Ana Velitchkova, 'Rationalization of Belonging: Transnational Community Endurance', *International Sociology* 36, no. 3 (2021): 419–38.

24 Scholarship on Esperanto in Bulgaria is scarce and mainly focuses on the post-Second World War period; see Ana Velitchkova, 'Nationalized Cosmopolitanism with Communist Characteristics: The Esperanto Movement's Survival Strategy in Post–World War II Bulgaria', *Social Science History* 46, no. 3 (2022): 617–42.

25 Ménil, *Tutmonda Jarlibro por 1904*, 65.

26 On other cases, such as Bohemia, see Bernhard Struck, 'Licht und Schatten im Esperantoland ohne Grenzen. Ein blinder Junge aus der Provinz, ein Eskimochef aus Mähren, ein Übersetzer aus England und Anarchisten in China', in *ZwischenWelten: Grenzüberschreitungen europäischer Geschichte*, ed. Katja Makhotina and Thomas Serrier (Darmstadt: Wissenschaftliche Buchgesellschaft, 2023), 269–82, here pp. 276–77.

27 Wenzlhuemer, 'The Dematerialization of Telecommunication, 21–2.

28 See Lajos Kökény and Vilmos Bleier, eds, *Enciklopedio de Esperanto* (Budapest: Literatura Mondo, 1933), 823.

29 See Kökény and Bleier, *Enciklopedio*, 220–22. On religion and the translation of the Bible, see Chapter 4.

30 Garvía, *Esperanto and Its Rivals*.

31 See Kökény and Bleier, *Enciklopedio de Esperanto,* 124, 130–34, 302, 391, 451. On the social transformations around 1900, see Philipp Blom, *The Vertigo Years: Change and Culture in the West, 1900–1914* (London: Weidenfeld & Nicolson, 2008), 193–203.

32 Hugo William Salokannel, *Biografiaro de l'Parencaro Salokannel* (Vaasa: Ikka, 1952). See also O'Keeffe, *Esperanto and Languages of Internationalism*, 68.

33 Garvía, *Esperanto and Its Rivals*, 103–11.

34 *Fervoja Esperantisto*, December, 1910, 3. On the periodical *Ruslanda Esperantisto*, see O'Keeffe, *Esperanto and Languages of Internationalism*, 61.

35 John Beveridge Collection, Ms36242/123.

36 Kökény and Bleier, *Enciklopedio*, 219; Oskar Levertin, 'Shylock. Poemo de O. Levertin, esperantigis Hj. J. Runeberg,' *Finna Esperantisto*, 1909.

37 See also O'Keeffe, *Esperanto and Languages of Internationalism*, 73f.

38 John Beveridge Collection, Bev PM8201.S7B.

39 John Beveridge Collection, Ms36242/117. See also Aleksander Bolesław Brzostowksi, ed., *Adresaro de Polaj Esperantistoj por 1909* (Warsaw: Jan Günther, 1909), 35.

40 John Beveridge Collection, Ms36242/175, Ms36242/199 and Ms36242/176, respectively.

41 John Beveridge Collection, Ms36242/165, Ms36242/166, Ms36242/120 and Ms36242/195, respectively.

42 John Beveridge Collection, Ms36242/112.

43 John Beveridge Collection, Ms36242/122.

44 Stanisłav Kamarýt, *Historio de la Esperanto-Movado en Ĉehoslovakio: Iom da Historio kaj Iom da Rememoroj* (Prague: Ĉeha Esperanto-Asocio, 1983).

45 Ziko Marcus Sikosek, *Sed Homoj kun Homoj: Universalaj Kongresoj de Esperanto, 1905–2005* (Rotterdam: Universala Esperanto-Asocio, 2005).

46 See George Marcus, 'Ethnography in/of the World System: The Emergence of Multi-Sited Ethnography', *Annual Review of Anthropology* 24 (1995): 95–117.

Chapter 2

From learning the language to founding local clubs: the making of an Esperanto speaker

When John Beveridge received postcards from his pen pals from Kymi, Harmanli and Hradec Králové around 1908, he had been an Esperanto speaker for three years. Soon after, in 1910, he was elected president of the Scottish Esperanto Federation. During his presidency, the annual Scottish Esperanto Congress took place in his hometown Dundee and, in 1912, he travelled to Kraków to attend the Eighth Universal Congress of Esperanto. Many years later, in May 1937, then eighty years old, John Beveridge gave a church service in Esperanto in Dunfermline, Scotland.[1] For over three decades, he devoted his time and energy to the cause of Esperanto.

Like him, two of his daughters – Lois and Heather Beveridge – learned the language and used it to participate in congresses, host Esperanto speakers from other countries in their family home and travel abroad. And so did people in nearby places like Montrose, a few miles north on the Scottish east coast, and in Perth, further inland from Dundee. However, why did these people, born and raised in predominantly monolingual settings in Scotland, decide to go through the process of studying this constructed language? Upon learning Esperanto, what did they do with it, considering that not many people in their surroundings could speak it? Asking these questions, this chapter examines the process of becoming an Esperanto speaker. Written around – rather than about – John Beveridge, the chapter analyses the artefacts he left behind in his journey of becoming an Esperanto speaker to reconstruct what this process looked like, as well as what places, people, things and encounters it involved.

Here we ask: what makes an Esperanto speaker? The notion of 'making' though has multiple meanings for our interests and analytical purposes. It certainly begins with learning the language. Yet, once the language is learned, a pressing question emerges: what next? In the case of a constructed language, the 'what next' is a key question. Unlike vernacular languages, Esperanto lacks a bounded territorial space where it is officially or customarily spoken. In contrast to people's first languages, there is no intergenerational language transmission or organic reproduction of an Esperanto-speaking community.[2] This chapter, therefore, is about this intricate 'what next'. Becoming an Esperanto speaker may involve primarily learning the language, but remaining an Esperanto speaker requires becoming invested in creating occasions on which the language can be used – in other words, becoming part and parcel of the constant process of (re)making and (re)animating this language community through persistent communicative exchanges.[3]

Firstly, retracing the steps of John, Lois and Heather Beveridge, we reconstruct, how they learned Esperanto – which takes us to autodidactic language learning materials, evening classes and cultural gatherings in hotels and conference venues around Dundee. Secondly, we pivot away from Dundee to other Scottish towns where Esperanto clubs took root, such as Perth, Arbroath, Aberdeen, Montrose, Kilmarnock and Linlithgow. These towns, each with only a few thousand inhabitants, were neither major cities nor cultural hubs. They rarely made the headlines of newspapers and never hosted one of the large and vibrant Universal Congresses of Esperanto. So, why read about the history of Esperanto in Dundee or Perth? We argue that it is only through looking at these easily overlooked places that we can reveal the backbone of the Esperanto-speaking community in the early twentieth century. It is this scale that allows us to uncover the grassroots level of this community, how it was built and made by ordinary people who devoted significant time and effort to constantly create occasions for the language to be effectively used in its spoken and written forms. Thus, by focusing on the local and regional Scottish level, this chapter approaches elements of the history of international communication from a novel perspective – one that turns language politics and the use of communication technologies at the time on their head.

International auxiliary languages were designed and promoted with the aim of fostering mutual understanding across borders, particularly among people from different national, ethnic and linguistic backgrounds.[4] Along these lines, enthusiastic promoters of international auxiliary languages would expect Esperanto to gain prominence amidst international, multilingual hubs such as Paris, London or Kraków. Similar expectations were shared by those invested in language policy through organisations such as the France-based Delegation for the Adoption of an International Auxiliary Language and the US-based International Auxiliary Language Association. Likewise, numerous technology enthusiasts who celebrated the progress symbolised by electricity at the 1893 World Exhibition in Chicago[5] – as well as innovators imagining the future of communication and mobility following the invention of the aeroplane – envisioned a world in which Esperanto, alongside the telephone, diesel locomotives and air travel, would serve as a vital tool for uniting a rapidly globalising world.

By contrast, Esperanto seemed to have gained ground primarily in small places, commonly perceived as 'isolated' and marginalised in historical accounts of international communication – places where internationalism, multilingualism and globalisation appeared irredeemably out of reach. Perhaps precisely for these reasons – and this is the key hypothesis this chapter engages with – inhabitants of these places were eager to learn a language like Esperanto and engage with some form of cross-border exchange. However, they did so mostly by remaining at the local level.

This chapter follows John Beveridge and his two daughters to analyse what it takes to become an Esperanto speaker. We examine the processes of learning and practising the language, attending Esperanto gatherings, organising cultural events and running local Esperanto clubs. This chapter explores the foundation of the Dundee Esperanto Club and its ties with other groups, which ranged from Esperanto groups nearby to chapters of the temperance movement. Lastly, we unpack how John Beveridge became one of the founders of the Scottish Esperanto Federation, being invested in breathing life again and again into the local enactments of the Esperanto-speaking community.

Narrating this history from the standpoint of small places in Scotland enables us to substantiate how ordinary people effectively engaged with international communication in the early twentieth century. They might not have been among the first ones to travel on an aeroplane or have a landline in their homes, but that does not mean they were isolated.

This also provides a fresh look at how, without the countless unsung heroes, early adopters, local activists and makers and shakers – of whom John Beveridge is simply one example – we would most likely not be speaking about Esperanto in the twenty-first century. In this regard, shifting the historiography of constructed languages and Esperanto from Zamenhof's Warsaw to small-town Scotland allows a novel entryway to our key questions: why would people devote their time and energy to study such a language and, once they learned it, what came next? Unlike Zamenhof, who envisaged Esperanto as a linguistic solution to problems of xenophobia and linguistic imperialism, what problem – if any – could make Esperanto meaningful in these arguably isolated places?

The first meeting in Dundee: setting the scene for the 'nova lingvo'

In 1905–6, Esperanto was under the spotlight and in the news. Hundreds of newspapers across Europe covered the story of Esperanto speakers gathering at the first international congress in Boulogne-sur-Mer, France, in 1905. Thousands of articles from tsarist Russia to Austria–Hungary, France and Spain created a buzz around this new language.[6] A sense of excitement was in the air and, as in many other places, the local press in Dundee picked up on it. This happened in the wake of the second international congress in Geneva, where 900 Esperanto speakers and 'representatives of 18 different languages' gathered in August 1906.[7] In October 1906, the *Dundee Advertiser* and other local papers reported about the 'nova lingvo' (new language) and the formation of an Esperanto club in the city.

It was Janette King (1862–1947) who presided over the inaugural meeting of the Dundee Esperanto Club at the Lamb's Hotel in October 1906. According to the local press, the meeting was 'largely attended', with King giving a lecture on the history of 'universal languages', Esperanto and the recently held congress in Geneva. 'Emboldened by the attendance before her' as well as the interest in the language, King 'formally moved the founding of an Esperanto club'. A committee, with Janette King as its first president, was voted in on the same evening. Others in the audience, including John Beveridge, expressed an interest in joining the newly formed club:

> Rev. John Beveridge [. . .] expressed his belief in the usefulness of Esperanto, remarking how awkward it was at international

> congresses to have the proceedings interpreted to the delegates. He also expressed his interest in the Club, and mentioned that, though he would not himself be able to be present on Wednesday evenings, he would be represented by members of the family.[8]

These family members were his daughters Lois and Heather Beveridge. In 1902, there had been an attempt to form an Esperanto club in the city, but it did not get off the ground. In 1906, by contrast, the initiative was a success. This time, members of the newly formed club did not waste any time and started meeting the following Wednesday at the Cercle Français, in Dundee City Centre. The local *Dundee Courier* regularly reported on the club's social events and gatherings, which drew between twenty and fifty participants.[9] With the Dundee club established and running, Scotland had three Esperanto clubs: both Glasgow's and Edinburgh's were founded in 1903, and others would follow in the coming years.

In 1905 and 1906, new Esperanto clubs were formed across Britain, including Birmingham, Bradford, Bristol, Chester, Deal, Goole, Kingston upon Thames, Manchester, Norwich and Sheffield – to name just a few. Dundee was a typical club in that it followed the wave of Esperanto enthusiasm in the aftermath of the first two congresses, along with the prospect of the third international congress to be held in Cambridge in 1907. A myriad of new clubs were founded in France, Germany, Austria–Hungary and beyond Europe.[10] Esperanto took root in a wide variety of places. Some were capital cities, others were bustling trade hubs, others were intellectual centres, home to universities.

Dundee was one of the fastest growing cities in Britain in the second half of the nineteenth century. Between 1851 and 1901, its population tripled from around 61,000 to over 182,000 inhabitants. By 1900, it had overtaken Aberdeen and was the third largest city in Scotland.[11] The rapid urbanisation and economic boom largely rested on Dundee's jute industry, which linked the port city to Bengal, where the raw jute fibres were harvested. Dundee textiles were shipped across the globe, to places in the British Empire, the European continent and the US. Other key industrial sectors in Dundee were shipbuilding and the whaling industry, but it was mainly the jute industry that carried with it the prolonged boom and rapid growth.[12]

There was a constant influx of workers to Dundee's industries, the majority of whom were women. Dundee was known as the 'women's town' as it pulled in a large female workforce from across Britain.[13] Given the significant surplus of women in Dundee, many of these – often young – were unmarried and lived together in shared accommodation. Dundee expanded rapidly through the immigration of workers, but housing was hard to come by and living conditions for workers were often poor. The lives of these women did not quite conform to what was frequently conveyed about young women during Victorian times: they were hard-working manual labourers, many were politically minded and went on strikes fighting for better wages and working conditions, and some were activists in the then growing women's rights movements.[14]

It was in this urban setting that the foundational meeting of the Dundee Esperanto Club took place. As with many other Esperanto clubs, its meetings and evening courses were held in spaces such as community halls, cafés and hotels. In Dundee, the first meeting took place in the Lamb's Hotel, part of a hotel business across Scotland run by Alexander Crawford Lamb (1843–97), as well as part of the wider temperance movement of the nineteenth century.[15]

It may not have been by sheer coincidence that the would-be Esperanto learners met at a temperance hotel. With its hard-working jute spinners, weavers, whalers and ship crews, Dundee most certainly had an alcohol problem.[16] The temperance movement was present locally – John Beveridge, for instance, was 'an ardent advocate of total abstinence'[17] – but it was also a widespread transnational political group. The early Esperanto-speaking community partly overlapped with the temperance movement as Esperanto offered – at least potentially – a language solution to such a cross-border organisation.[18] More generally, the language appealed to reform movements, philanthropic organisations and international Christian organisations, ranging from the Rotary Club to the YMCA.[19]

In this urban setting marked by local iterations of broader international issues ranging from women's rights and workers' rights to temperance, Janette King gave her pitch for Esperanto. King was one of the first women journalists in Scotland around 1900, having worked since 1881 for the *Dundee Advertiser* and, later, for the *Evening Telegraph*. In her journalistic work, she covered workers' rights and mill strikes in Dundee, while also advocating for women's rights and universal suffrage. She was engaged in the local temperance movement and was a co-founder of the Dundee branch of the Women's Liberal Federation. In her line of work, the news and buzz around Esperanto certainly did not escape her. Even though she does not seem to have attended the earliest Universal Congresses of Esperanto,[20] her contacts with fellow journalists abroad and her local activism for transnational causes such as women's rights and temperance turned Esperanto into a logical and consequential interest to her.

As only one of countless women that took on leading activist roles and helped launch clubs, Janette King acted as the first president of the Dundee Esperanto Club before she and her husband moved to Newcastle the following year, with John Beveridge taking over as president in 1908. As with any other organisation or society, one needs Kings and Beveridges, the rank-and-file members who do more than just pay an annual membership fee and turn up every now and then. In Esperantujo, this is no different: as the next section will show, becoming an active Esperanto speaker also involved creating the occasions and the institutional frameworks that would host the learning and regular use of the language.

Becoming an Esperanto speaker: learning, writing, congregating

Once someone decides to learn Esperanto – motivated by various reasons – the first step in the making of an Esperanto speaker is studying the language. In John Beveridge's case this involved working through a number of self-study learning materials and manuals. These included books he owned, such as *Esperanto for Beginners* – a low-cost publication by the British Esperanto Association – *The Esperanto Home-Student*, *Esperanto for All: How to Read, Write and Speak It* and *A Grammar and Commentary on the International Language Esperanto*,[21] as well as other works on grammar and syntax.[22]

These learning materials sought to present Esperanto as a language appealing to broad and diverse publics. Their underlying message was unequivocal: becoming an Esperanto speaker was for anyone. The preface to *An Esperanto Grammar and Commentary*, for instance, praised the language for enabling 'anyone to correspond on any topic, social, commercial, or scientific, with persons of all nationalities'. The author, George Cox, highlighted the growing body of translations covering various topics and disciplines, in particular the sciences and medicine.[23] Like many other self-learning books, Cox's volume runs learners through the alphabet and its pronunciation before delving into grammar followed by exercises, specimen texts and basic vocabulary. While all the materials emphasised the ease of learning Esperanto, Cox aimed to equip beginners to 'write and speak it in good style', noting that, like 'every national language, [Esperanto possessed] a certain style and elegance of expression of its own'.[24]

The appeal for anyone to become an Esperanto speaker was indeed broad and socially inclusive. Print runs were high – for instance, James Robbie's *Esperanto Home-Student*, originally published in 1909, was in its sixth edition with a total of 25,000 copies by 1913. The low price of just one or two pennies per copy further reflected its accessibility. Robbie's slim volume of around fifty pages was aimed at self-learners and evening school students, and it targeted learners from a wide spectrum of professional backgrounds – from pharmacists, lawyers and teachers to bankers, sailors and manual labourers. Some professions – such as railwaymen, postal employees and policemen – were singled out as having their own Esperanto magazines. Robbie concluded his book's opening remarks with an explicit invitation, particularly aimed at manual labourers interested in the language: 'Are YOU interested in the objects which any of the above Societies have at heart? Then, Become an ESPERANTIST, and enter into communion with kindred fellow labourers all over the world.'[25]

Part of the language-learning process, as well as of the consolidation of Esperanto beyond its grammar and syntax, drew on a rapid increase in both translated literature and works originally written in Esperanto. Beveridge himself owned works including Lewis Carroll's *Alice in Wonderland* translated as *La aventuroj de Alico en Mirlando* and Esperanto translations of Charles Dickens and August Strindberg.[26] In addition, Beveridge had numerous issues of Esperanto magazines including *Germana Esperanto-Gazeto*, *Amerika Esperantisto* and *Brazila Revuo Esperantista*, as well as magazines from Austria–Hungary, Finland and France – several of which he received in exchange for posting British Esperanto magazines abroad to his pen pals.

The vast majority of Esperanto literature, language learning and propaganda materials found in the Beveridge household date from the period between 1906 and 1913, when the family lived in Dundee. However, even when the family relocated to a small parish in Fossoway – a village located between Perth and Edinburgh – John Beveridge continued collecting Esperanto magazines and literature. Later, after moving further inland to lead a parish in Gartmore – and, therefore, being seemingly more geographically isolated from the Esperanto scene – he nevertheless continued to be a regular presence at Esperanto gatherings.[27] Having these reading materials at hand and on his desk, John Beveridge also kept an exercise book in which he drafted some of his congress talks and magazine publication drafts.[28]

In a language that was more regularly written than spoken, reading magazines was a key way of widening one's vocabulary. As part of a language community largely based on sharing printed materials, copies of periodicals were sent abroad or exchanged with pen pals, as John Beveridge did when he received magazines from Brazil or Finland in exchange for a copy of *The British Esperantist*.[29]

Early Esperanto periodicals served to showcase the language in use and the consolidation of this community. Many of these publications, from *The British Esperantist* to the *Germana Esperanto-Gazeto*, were bilingual in the early decades of Esperanto, to attract newcomers and support those still learning the language. While some articles appeared only in Esperanto or English (or German), most of the content was available in bilingual format, often in dual-language columns. Having the two languages side by side allowed for accessible reading practice.

With news about newly found clubs, forthcoming congresses, the latest Esperanto publications and adverts for shops where one could find Esperanto books and learning materials, as well as sections with lists of addresses of pen pals, these print media were among the spaces through which the first generation of Esperanto learners joined the language community. Over the years, John Beveridge became a regular contributor to *The British Esperantist* and *La Revuo*. Like her father, Lois Beveridge also contributed to Esperanto magazines. She was eighteen years old when one of her poems was published in *The British Esperantist* – in 1908, the same year she travelled to Dresden to attend that year's Universal Congress of Esperanto.[30]

Esperanto speakers became familiar with one another by reading each other's names on the pages of magazines and by meeting in person at both local and international gatherings. When Lois Beveridge travelled to Dresden, she likely had the opportunity to put faces to names she had previously encountered through her readings – figures such as Ludwik Zamenhof and Marie Hankel.

Marie Hankel (1844–1929) – to whom we will return in Chapter 3 – was a prolific early writer of Esperanto literary prose and poetry. She was highly active in the local Esperanto scene in Dresden, where she lived. Having come to Esperanto in the same period as the Beveridges, Hankel became the first president of the Esperantista Literatura Asocio (Esperanto Literature Association) in 1911. At the time John Beveridge served as president of the Scottish Esperanto Federation.

Marie Hankel and Lois Beveridge may or may not have met in Dresden, yet the lives of Marie Hankel and the Beveridges significantly overlapped. In addition to their leadership roles in Esperantujo, both Marie Hankel and John Beveridge had articles published in the same issue of *La Revuo*. Among Marie Hankel's short stories and poems was a piece she published in commemoration of the German humorist and writer Wilhelm Busch (1832–1908).[31] On the same page of the literary magazine was an obituary written by John Beveridge in honour of the mathematician Lord William Kelvin (1824–1907).[32]

Just as with many other Esperanto speakers at the time, Lois Beveridge, Marie Hankel and John Beveridge had mastered the language to a level of proficiency well beyond passive reading or the odd icebreaker in classroom conversations. They translated and published literary prose and poetry, as well as content of general interest to a wider readership – and they did so as volunteers, with no direct payback or monetary incentive. Regardless of having ever met in person, Hankel and the Beveridges certainly met one another on paper.

None of these activities and encounters would have been possible without the underbelly of hundreds of local clubs like the ones in Dundee and Dresden. These often-unacknowledged local clubs were responsible for the heavy work of promoting the language, arranging the teaching and sales of learning materials, and congregating at the local level. Most importantly, local clubs also tailored Esperanto to the demands and interests of people whose lives had little in common with Zamenhof's in 1887 Warsaw. Relatedly, the Universal Congresses of Esperanto – short-lived events for a few summer days every year – would perhaps not have existed without the support of local clubs who, ultimately, were the ones responsible for inviting and hosting these large-scale materialisations of Esperantujo.

After Janette King moved to Newcastle, a certain Alexander Pride took over as president of the Dundee Esperanto Club, preceding John Beveridge's presidency in 1908. That year, *The British Esperantist* reported that the club was 'still small in point of numbers, but the members are enthusiasts and are hopeful of gaining new converts'.[33] On other occasions, the Dundee press praised the 'local Esperanto success' when both Alexander Pride and Lois Beveridge gained, through examination, the British Esperanto Association's advanced diploma in language proficiency. Holders of this diploma, the article explained, were recognised teachers able to organise language exams in the district. 'With Esperantists in Dundee qualified to act as examiners, it is probable that the number of candidates for the diploma will be much larger in the future.'[34]

In the years that followed, the Dundee club indeed flourished, with numerous regular events. One of these was held on 9 April 1912 at the Lamb's Hotel, where everything had started a few years earlier. That evening, the club's president invited members for *tetrinkado, kantoj, deklamoj* and *babilado*. Coming together for tea, singing, literary recitations, an evening lecture or simply an informal chat constituted a typical evening in any Esperanto club. From social gatherings to outings – involving picnics, excursions and visits to Esperanto clubs in places nearby – Esperanto clubs brought together men and women, younger people like the Beveridge daughters and older demographics, as well as people from a variety of professional backgrounds, including clergymen, solicitors, journalists and librarians.

The Beveridge family was actively involved in these early club activities, turning the practices of getting together and congregating into part and parcel of their local experience of Esperantujo. A social gathering in 1908 included the songs *La Espero* – the anthem of Esperanto – and *Serenade* sung by Heather Beveridge, and the song *Mia Esperantistino* performed by John Beveridge. Along with Heather Beveridge, three other either young or unmarried women – indicated as 'F-ino' and, thus, as Miss in the programme – also performed that evening.[35]

Such evenings were first and foremost social. They certainly served the purpose of language practice, but they were also about building relationships, being together and having fun. Amidst conversations that constantly switched between Esperanto, English and, occasionally, Scots, there must have been laughter over debates about how to say such and such words in Esperanto, which suffix to use and why the Esperanto word for 'shelf' was *breto*, rather than the more English-friendly *ŝelfo**.

Like in chess clubs or book clubs, conversations and events in the Esperanto club did not necessarily revolve around Esperanto. Rather, chess, books and Esperanto were primarily the means and motivators for people to join a local club, come together on a regular basis and do things with people with whom they might become friends. Coming home from such events, some may have felt inspired to do more with the language, such as writing poetry, exchanging correspondence with Esperanto speakers abroad or even travel to a congress – or, in some cases, simply go along to the next social gathering of the club.

Why only spread the word when we could also travel and have fun?

The Dundee club was by no means exceptional in shaping the local materialisations of Esperantujo. However, it was a particularly successful one, with constant activities and a steady membership rising to around one hundred members by around 1910.[36] While Esperanto speakers expected the language to connect people from distant places and across borders, Esperanto connected people at the local level in the first place.

In 1908, a group of people from Perth – some thirty kilometres further inland from Dundee, along the River Tay – reached out for support to create a local Esperanto club, seeking advice on how to reproduce Dundee's success. The person chosen to be the link between the two places was Lois Beveridge – after all, she was one of the few certified Esperanto teachers at the time. Young and active, Lois Beveridge soon found herself commuting between Dundee and Perth to run weekly evening classes and help organise social events.[37]

A photograph taken in 1908 captures the Perth Esperanto Club at the time – a group of twenty-eight adults and one child gathered in a park (Figure 2.1). Precisely half of the group is made up of women, which was not unusual for Esperanto clubs at the time. The people in the photograph appear dressed for the occasion: men wearing suits and hats, women wearing long dresses, most of them with white blouses and hats – some of which were elaborate and unlike people's everyday attire. Despite being staged, this photograph shows an air of spontaneous joy: people are smiling, with some sheepish grins and open laughter. While Esperanto was conceived as a serious response to ethnolinguistic tensions, aimed at fostering cross-border understanding, this image from Perth reflects the more personal, communal pleasures of Esperanto life. Photographs from other locations during this period capture a comparable atmosphere of warmth, conviviality and shared enthusiasm around the language.[38]

In addition to language classes, the Perth Esperanto Club organised social evenings similar to those in Dundee. On Christmas Eve in 1908, the club celebrated the end of the year with a *Festkunveno* (Festive Gathering). The somewhat makeshift, handwritten programme consisted of talks, committee reports, a violinist and a juggler for entertainment. Lois Beveridge gave a talk on her experiences at the Universal Congress in Dresden earlier

Figure 2.1: The Perth Esperanto Club, c. 1908. Source: John Beveridge Collection, Ms38908/17. Courtesy of the University of St Andrews Libraries and Museums, ID: ms36242-ms36244

that year. The leaflet with the programme also contained the lyrics of *La Espero*, the Esperanto anthem that became a fixture of such festive events.[39]

Likewise, a *Sociala Kunveno* (Social Gathering) held at Perth's Royal George Hotel on the evening of 15 February 1912, in tribute to Zamenhof's birthday, included musical performances, dances – from waltz to a sword dance and quadrilles – a violin performance, magical entertainment, cards and table games, as well as a running buffet. Beyond simply learning the language and occasionally exchanging correspondence, many Esperanto speakers saw these social activities as alluring motives driving them to regularly use the language. Along these lines, the longer-term success of such clubs relied on the constant remaking of such activities and gatherings. From the programmes of social evenings that survived time, Esperanto speakers certainly knew how to have fun and organise enjoyable evenings.

By the time the Perth Esperanto Club was formed, *The British Esperantist* reported on activities of clubs in Edinburgh, Glasgow and Leith, which had also been founded in the first decade of 1900. Edinburgh's club boasted a membership of 320 and was growing steadily. The Glasgow club was 'actively engaged in propaganda and study. The president's class is progressing well, and the weekly club meetings are a great success. A special feature of these meetings is the reading in Esperanto of papers on various literary subjects.'[40] The latter included, for instance, lectures in Esperanto on Charles Dickens and Scottish poetry, which attracted up to 200 attendees.

In the first decade of the twentieth century, Glasgow had a population of over 775,000 inhabitants, and Edinburgh's population was close to 400,000. Esperanto clubs flourished in both cities, with membership figures comparable to those in continental European cities. Dresden – which hosted the 1908 Universal Congress of Esperanto – boasted a thriving Esperanto scene, while Prague, with a population of around 200,000, was home to around ten Esperanto clubs at the time.

Similar patterns of producing and reproducing the Esperanto community at the local level can be traced in many places across Europe. For instance, similar to what the Beveridge family did in Dundee, Julie Šupichová (1884–1970) – a young teacher, from the same generation as the Beveridge daughters – launched an Esperanto circle in her hometown, Červený Kostelec, a town in Bohemia of around 8,000 inhabitants. A few years later, in 1910, upon moving to Prague, she founded another Esperanto Circle, which she led for several years. In addition to founding clubs and producing Esperanto learning materials for Czech speakers, Julie Šupichová served as the secretary of the 1921 Universal Congress of Esperanto, held in Prague – the congress that marked the resurgence of annual international congresses following the interruption caused by the First World War.[41]

The dissemination of this international auxiliary language in big cities with international trade, as well as in cultural and intellectual hubs like Edinburgh, Dresden and Prague, was perhaps not a surprise. After all, these were places where the appeal of a language aimed at international communication felt especially immediate and relevant. Yet the reach of Esperanto and the (re)production of Esperantujo extended well beyond these urban centres into smaller towns and their hinterlands. In this regard, Scotland serves here as a case in point to spotlight a broader phenomenon also happening in places such as southern Finland, Bulgaria and eastern Bohemia, as Chapter 1 hinted at.

By 1910, several new clubs had mushroomed across Scotland. What started in Dundee and spread to Perth was repeated in coastal places like Arbroath, Montrose, St Andrews and, further north, in Aberdeen. Montrose at the time had a population of around 12,000, and Arbroath, just over

22,000.[42] These towns – as well as smaller villages such as Cowdenbeath and Burntisland, north of Edinburgh – were not key cultural hubs, did not host major trade activities and had no key industries. Yet, Esperanto drew the attention and spoke to the interests of people in these places.

The consolidation of local Esperanto clubs was not always easy. In some places, like Aberdeen (150,000 inhabitants), it took several attempts to form a functioning club. Similar to Dundee, an early attempt at it around 1904 failed. It was a later visit by London-based, experienced Esperanto speaker John Bredall – who gave a 'very convincing presentation of his case, which aroused great enthusiasm' – that eventually boosted the formation of a club, with evening classes promptly attracting fifty learners.[43]

How much the success – or sheer survival – of such a club rested on the efforts of one or two very engaged individuals was stressed by David S. Rattray, a local Esperanto speaker who penned, in English, a brief account of the Aberdeen club:

> A special tribute must be paid to the good work done by Miss Constance Ogston [who taught the language and organised most outings] who has kept the flag flying through circumstances of great discouragement and difficulty which might well have been fatal to the Esperanto career of one less enthusiastic, courageous, and persevering. Valuable help has also been given by Miss Annie L. Burgess, our esteemed secretary & treasurer, who is the first student of our group to gain the Diploma of the British Esperanto Association, and who in all her work for Esperanto has displayed the qualities of the true pioneer.[44]

If it was not for efforts such as those of Constance Ogston to gain a teaching qualification and pass the language on to newcomers, or Lois Beveridge to teach in Perth, or Annie Burgess to keep the books and minutes of her local club, or Julie Šupichová to found a new group wherever she lived, Esperantujo would perhaps never have been institutionalised.

In his brief account of the development of Esperanto in Scotland, John Beveridge analysed some of the obstacles in the process of building the Esperanto community. First, 'Scotland has not had so much diversity of language to contend with as many other lands.'[45] In other words, language diversity at the local and regional levels did not constitute a challenge as it did elsewhere, as Scotland did not offer a contentious scenario where people from different linguistic backgrounds struggled to communicate or clashed with each other. John Beveridge also contended that Scottish people had followed the rise as much as the collapse of Volapük as an earlier international auxiliary language project in the 1880s, which made some of them rather reticent about the prospects of Esperanto. Yet, according to him, the Scots were eager to travel abroad. The potential of going beyond their localities – be it via correspondence exchange or congress attendance – were among the key reasons driving people from these small towns and villages to organise and participate in events that would turn them into fully fledged Esperanto speakers.

Dundee's 1911 Scottish Congress and Kraków's 1912 Universal Congress: being at home abroad

In 1912, it was finally John Beveridge's turn to travel. Four years after his daughter Lois attended the 1908 Universal Congress in Dresden, he set off for the Universal Congress of Esperanto in Kraków. Formerly the capital of Poland and, at the time, part of Austria–Hungary, Kraków had been chosen to host the congress in celebration of Esperanto's Polish origins twenty-five years after Ludwik Zamenhof's first publication. As for many others who had the opportunity to attend such large gatherings, visiting a Universal Congress of Esperanto surely was the highlight of John Beveridge's long-standing engagement with the language (Figure 2.2).

In previous years, John Beveridge had helped found and then presided over the local club in Dundee. He also established a wide network of pen pals, sent back and forth Esperanto materials, exchanged friendly postcards and postal stamps, published in Esperanto periodicals and participated in translating the New Testament. In the latter process, he also exchanged postcards with Ludwik Zamenhof, and the congress in Kraków would constitute the only opportunity for the two to ever meet in person.[46] However, meeting Zamenhof was not the reason for his trip. John Beveridge's main purpose was to experience a Universal Congress in action, be part of it and, ultimately, propose, on behalf of the Scottish Esperanto Federation, to host a Universal Congress in Edinburgh in the near future.

The Scottish Esperanto Federation was one of the key spaces in which John Beveridge played a leading role. Two years before the Kraków congress, in 1910, John Beveridge became the founding president of the Federation. In 1911, he took on the role of vice-president, with J. D. Simpson – a founding member of the Montrose club – becoming president. The

Figure 2.2: Group photograph at the Eighth Universal Congress of Esperanto, in Kraków, 1912. Source: Historical Museum of the City of Kraków, MHK-Fs12663/IX

Federation was organised in four districts – *Norda* (north), *Centra* (central), *Okcidenta* (west) and *Orienta* (east) – each with its own secretary. Overall, fifteen clubs were affiliated with the newly founded Federation, which featured a total of 531 Esperanto-speaking members. Whereas the Esperanto clubs in Edinburgh and Glasgow boasted the largest membership figures, it was John Beveridge's home district in east Scotland that was singled out as the most active and vibrant region.[47]

The main purpose of the Scottish Esperanto Federation was to further promote the language and institutionalise the language community by replicating at the national level the model of founding new clubs, gaining members and garnering new learners. The first annual report listed among the Federation's goals to foster the foundation of new clubs in Aberdeen, Inverness, Crieff, Cupar, Angus, Forfar, Arbroath and Oban. While new clubs in Aberdeen and Arbroath did come into being, this is less certain in other locations. As part of this strategy of founding clubs, the meetings of the Federation's steering committee were tactically held in small Scottish villages where there were no Esperanto clubs yet.[48]

The foundation of the Scottish Esperanto Federation mimicked at the national level what had been achieved in 1908 – two years earlier – at the transnational level, with the establishment of the World Esperanto Association, then headquartered in Geneva. Between the local and the transnational level, many other national associations were founded during this period to coordinate activities and institutionalise the growing Esperanto community.

Even preceding the formal establishment of the Scottish Esperanto Federation, the most active members of several local clubs regularly gathered to organise the Scottish Congresses of Esperanto held in Stirling (1906), Linlithgow (1907), Edinburgh (1908) and Perth (1909). It was during the 1910 Scottish Congress in Glasgow that the Scottish Federation came into being. With John Beveridge as its first president, the following Scottish congress would be held in Dundee.

Leading up to the June 1911 congress in Dundee, the secretary of the Scottish Federation announced that the coming congress would 'be the most interesting and important Scottish Congress yet held'.[49] The congress's honorary presidents were John Pollen – then President of the British Esperanto Association – and, more prominently, Winston Churchill (1874–1965) as Home Secretary and Alexander Wilkie (1850–1929) as Member of Parliament for Dundee. In addition to attracting people – both Esperanto speakers and non-speakers curious about the potential of the language – such congresses also attracted the attention of the press, as well as constituting opportunities for Esperanto to gain the favour of political authorities.

The 1911 congress in Dundee included talks and debates on topics ranging from Esperanto in medicine and the commercial world to the potential of Esperanto in the Red Cross, in peace movements, in missionary work and among the blind. Close to John Beveridge's heart and practical commitments, there was also a session to report on the translation of the Bible into Esperanto.[50] Aside from one of the opening speeches as president of the Federation, John Beveridge led the church service on the Sunday of the congress.

In addition to these more formal activities, the congress programme also featured teatime gatherings, dinners, songs, dances, a theatrical performance and visits to the city's Victoria Art Galleries. These activities were conducted entirely in Esperanto, which was the key feature that made national and international congresses the highlight of many people's experience with the language. For a period of four days in Dundee (16–19 June 1911) or eight days in Kraków (11–18 August 1912), Esperanto speakers could almost completely step out of their linguistic comfort zones and daily routines – carried out in regional or national languages – to join a language community whose membership constituted an entirely separate facet of their life experiences.

During Esperanto congresses, the everyday work commitments of a clergyman or journalist lost their centrality as they engaged in voluntary, collective efforts to perform a theatre play, just as solicitors set aside their office work to act as tour guides showing Esperanto speakers around a local art gallery. Speaking Esperanto constituted the cue to temporarily leave behind one's everyday concerns in order to participate in a microcosm founded on egalitarianism, voluntary work, creativity and a heightened sense of community.

One of the main outcomes of the Dundee congress was to lay the foundation for the Federation to propose Edinburgh as the host city for the 1915 Universal Congress of Esperanto.[51] It was agreed that this proposal would be formally made at the following year's Universal Congress in Kraków. The honour to do so fell on John Beveridge. The 1913 annual report of the Scottish Esperanto Federation proudly announced that Edinburgh's invitation to host the 1915 congress had indeed been accepted at the 1913 Universal Congress of Esperanto held in Bern. The prospect of creating the highlight of the Esperanto experience in Scotland motivated local speakers to further teach the language, organise local activities and form clubs in preparation for this major event.

Concluding remarks

Not all members of the Dundee Esperanto Club and the Scottish Esperanto Federation were Beveridges, Hankels, Simpsons and Šupichovás. As with any club – be it a tennis or a book club – many members simply pay their membership fees and enjoy attending gatherings, without taking on additional responsibilities. Yet, such clubs exist because there are people who put time and energy into setting them up and running them. It was these volunteer presidents, treasurers and secretaries of local Esperanto clubs in the early twentieth century who ensured the spread of Esperanto and played a role in shaping this language community, providing speakers not only with reasons to learn the language but, most importantly, with opportunities to regularly use it.

Just as ordinary individuals – arguably more so than key figures like Ludwik Zamenhof – came to constitute the backbone of Esperantujo, it was at the local level that the foundations of Esperantujo were laid. Congresses alone, held only once a year, were not enough to ensure the long-term stability of a geographically dispersed Esperantujo. As John Beveridge's accounts illustrate, while crossing borders may be the ultimate goal for many people learning Esperanto, one does not normally live in a constant state of border-crossing. In this scenario, local Esperanto clubs provided opportunities to breathe life again and again into the language community throughout the year, between congresses.

In August 1914, as the First World War broke out, most cross-border Esperanto activities were interrupted, just as much international communication was disrupted in one way or another. As a consequence, the Universal Congress of Esperanto planned for Paris in 1914 was cancelled at the last minute and the one scheduled for Edinburgh did not take place in 1915.

What next? Reaching back to the question that opened this chapter, becoming an Esperanto speaker involves being committed to regularly create and join occasions on which to speak the language – and, in this manner, to constantly create and recreate the Esperanto-speaking community, particularly at the local level. By founding clubs, leading organisations, writing, publishing, exchanging correspondence and attending congresses, John Beveridge played his part in this community-building practice and made the most of what Esperanto had to offer.

Meanwhile, what comes next in the face of the First World War? The Universal Congress scheduled for Edinburgh did not take place in 1915, but the city did host a Universal Congress in 1926, after cross-border travelling had been fully resumed following the war. However, at a period in which international communication was heavily disrupted, it was the social gatherings at the local level – as well as personal correspondence and magazines – that kept the language alive and increasingly emphasised the potential of Esperanto in helping reunite, through an international auxiliary language, a divided world, at a time when nationalisms seemed to have triumphed over internationalism.

Notes

1 John Beveridge Collection, Ms36244/4.

2 Guilherme Fians, 'Mind the Age Gap: Communication Technologies and Intergenerational Language Transmission among Esperanto Speakers in France', *Language Problems and Language Planning* 44, no. 1 (2020): 87–108; Sabine Fiedler, 'Standardization and Self-Regulation in an International Speech Community: The Case of Esperanto', *International Journal of the Sociology of Language* 177 (2006): 67–90.

3 See Humphrey Tonkin, *Lingvo kaj popolo: Aktualaj problemoj de la Esperanto-movado* (Rotterdam: Universala Esperanto-Asocio, 2006).

4 Garvía, *Esperanto and Its Rivals*.

5 See K. G. Beauchamp, *Exhibiting Electricity* (London: The Institution of Electrical Engineers, 1997).

6 On newspaper coverage of Esperanto at the time, see the newspaper collection *Zeitungsausschnitte 1898–1915*, available at the Austrian National Library.

7 John Beveridge Collection, Ms38908/17.

8 John Beveridge Collection, Ms38908/17.

9 John Beveridge Collection, Ms38908/17.

10 Félicien de Ménil, ed. *Tutmonda Jarlibro Esperantista Enhavanta La Adresaron de Dro Zamenhof por 1907* (Paris: Hachette, 1907), 254–71.

11 Patricia Dennison, *The Evolution of Scotland's Towns: Creation, Growth and Fragmentation* (Edinburgh: Edinburgh University Press, 2022), 300; Michael Anderson, *Scotland's Populations from the 1850s to Today* (Oxford: Oxford University Press, 2018), 99.

12 Jim Tomlinson, *Dundee and the Empire: 'Juteopolis' 1850–1939* (Edinburgh: Edinburgh University Press, 2016); Tara Sethia, 'The Rise of the Jute Manufacturing Industry in Colonial India: A Global Perspective', *Journal of World History* 7, no. 1 (1996): 71–99.

13 Emma M. Wainwright, 'Constructing Gendered Workplace "Types": The Weaver-Millworker Distinction in Dundee's Jute Industry, c. 1880–1910', *Gender, Place & Culture* 14, no. 4 (2007): 467–9.

14 Eleanor Gordon, *Women and the Labour Movement in Scotland 1850–1914* (Oxford: Oxford University Press, 1991), 142; Alexandra Hughes-Johnson and Lyndsey Jenkins, eds., *The Politics of Women's Suffrage: Local, National and International Dimensions* (London: University of London Press, 2021).

15 John Kemp, 'Red Tayside? Political Change in Early Twentieth-Century Dundee', in Christopher Whatley and Bob Harris, eds., *Victorian Dundee: Image and Realities* (East Linton: Tuckwell, 2000), 217–39.

16 George B. Wilson, 'A Statistical Review of the Variations during the Last Twenty Years in the Consumption of Intoxicating Drinks in the United Kingdom, and in Convictions for Offences Connected with Intoxication, with Discussion of the Causes to Which These Variations May Be Ascribed', *Journal of the Royal Statistical Society* 75, no. 2 (1912): 183–247, here 231–2. George Bailey Wilson, *Alcohol and the Nation: A Contribution to the Study of the Liquor Problem in the United Kingdom from 1800 to 1935* (London: Nicholson and Watson, 1940), 293–5.

17 John Beveridge Collection, Ms36244/15, 2.

18 See, for instance, *The British Esperantist*, 3 March 1905, 41, on the formation of an Esperanto League by the Swedish Temperance Association to foster international cooperation. On the global temperance movement, see Nikolay Kamenov, *Global Temperance and the Balkans: American Missionaries, Swiss Scientists and Bulgarian Socialists, 1870–1940* (Cham: Palgrave Macmillan, 2020); Ian Tyrrell, *Woman's World, Woman's Empire: The Woman's Christian Temperance Union in International Perspective, 1880–1930* (Chapel Hill: University of North Carolina, 1991).

19 See, for instance, Harald Fischer-Tiné, Stefan Huebner and Ian Tyrrell, eds., *Spreading Protestant Modernity: Global Perspectives on the Social Work of the YMCA and YWCA, 1889–1970* (Honolulu: University of Hawai'i Press, 2021).

20 Universala Kongreso de Esperanto, *2a Universala Kongreso de Esperanto: Nomaro de la Kongresanoj* (Geneva: Universala Kongreso de Esperanto, 1907).

21 British Esperanto Association, *Esperanto for Beginners* (London: British Esperanto Association, n.d.); James Robbie, *The Esperanto Home-Student* (Edinburgh: Leith Burghs Pilot, 1913); British Esperanto Association, *Esperanto for All: How to Read, Write and Speak It* (London: British Esperanto Association, 1913); George Cox, *A Grammar and Commentary on the International Language Esperanto* (London: British Esperanto Association, 1914).

22 John Beveridge Collection, Bev PM8202.E8; 4; Bev PM8213.E8R7; Bev PM8213.C7. See, for instance, Paul Fruictier, *Esperanta sintakso laŭ verkoj de S-ro D-ro Zamenhof kaj aliaj aŭtoroj* (Paris: Hachette, 1907).

23 Cox, *Grammar and Commentary*, v.

24 Cox, *Grammar and Commentary*, vii–ix.

25 Robbie, *Esperanto Home-Student*, non-paginated.

26 See John Beveridge Collection, Bev PM8285.D6A5; Lewis Carroll, *La aventuroj de Alico en Mirlando*, trans. E. L. Kearney (London: British Esperanto Association, 1910).

27 John Beveridge Collection, Ms36244/15.

28 John Beveridge Collection, Ms36244/2b.

29 Benedict Anderson, *Imagined Communities: Reflections on the Origin and Spread of Nationalism* (London: Verso, 1991), 37–46; David Barton and Mary Hamilton, *Local Literacies: Reading and Writing in One Community* (London: Routledge, 2012).

30 Lois Beveridge, 'Eĉ pereos tio ĉi', *The British Esperantist*, March 1908, 43.

31 Marie Hankel, 'Wilhelm Busch', *La Revuo*, III, March 1908, 348–9.

32 John Beveridge, 'Barono Kelvin', *La Revuo*, III, March 1908, 347–8.

33 *The British Esperantist*, January 1908, 15. See also *Oficiala Gazeto Esperantista*, November 1908, 147.

34 John Beveridge Collection, Ms38908/17.

35 John Beveridge Collection, Ms38908/17.

36 John Beveridge Collection, Ms36244/15.

37 John Beveridge Collection, Ms36244/15.

38 See, for instance, photographs taken in 1908 of the Konversacia Esperantista Klubo in Copenhagen, available at the Austrian National Library, 1092 B, 24.3 C.

39 John Beveridge Collection, Ms38908/17.

40 *The British Esperantist*, January 1908, 15.

41 Stanislav Kamarýt, *Historio de la Esperanto-Movado en Ĉehoslovakio: Iom da historio kaj iom da rememoroj* (Prague: Ĉeha Esperanto-Asocio, 1983), 53–4.

42 Dennisson, *The Evolution of Scotland's Towns*, 300.

43 John Beveridge Collection, Ms36244/3.

44 John Beveridge Collection, Ms36244/5.

45 John Beveridge Collection, Ms36244/1.

46 John Beveridge Collection, Ms36242/169; Ms36242/223.

47 John Beveridge Collection, Ms38908/16.

48 John Beveridge Collection, Ms38908/16.

49 John Beveridge Collection, Ms38908/15.

50 John Beveridge Collection, Ms38908/15.

51 John Beveridge Collection, Ms38908/16.

Chapter 3

Gendered talk: Esperanto-speaking women and languages of egalitarianism

In August 1908, eighteen-year-old Lois Beveridge travelled from Dundee to Dresden, without her parents or any of her three siblings, to attend the Fourth Universal Congress of Esperanto. Upon returning, she gave a talk at the Esperanto club in Perth about her trip. Lois Beveridge was among the many women who attended Esperanto congresses abroad. Photographs – like the one from the 1912 Congress in Kraków, shown in Chapter 2 – and programmes of early twentieth-century Universal Congresses attest to the omnipresence of women in this language community. Like Lois Beveridge, Esperanto-speaking women shared their experiences abroad with local clubs after returning home, and were central to the maintenance, growth and spread of Esperantujo. In this chapter, these ubiquitous yet largely overlooked women of the early Esperanto community take centre stage.

Here we revisit a history of Esperanto that has often been written as a predominantly male affair. Ludwik Zamenhof was a man, and so were the founding fathers of most Esperanto clubs and editors of major Esperanto periodicals. Likewise, the earliest Esperanto authors and translators were primarily men. However, even a passing glance at sources from the period reveals that speaking Esperanto was far from an exclusively male endeavour. On the contrary, women taught the language, held prominent roles as presidents and vice-presidents of Esperanto clubs and also played leading roles in Universal Congresses of Esperanto.

Historians tend to acknowledge only two notable exceptions to this male dominance. The first is Lidia Zamenhof (1904–42), the youngest daughter of Ludwik Zamenhof. She became notorious for publishing original literature and translating into Esperanto both Polish literature and books from the Bahá'í Faith, consolidating what would become a long-standing connection between Esperanto and the Bahá'í Faith.[1] The second commonplace exception is Alice Vanderbilt Morris (1874–1950), who lent critical support to research on international auxiliary languages in the early days of Esperanto by founding the International Auxiliary Language Association (IALA) in the US and commissioning linguists like Edward Sapir and Otto Jespersen to explore the feasibility of such languages.[2]

By viewing Esperanto through the experiences of Lois Beveridge – an Esperanto teacher – and Heather Beveridge – a trained chemist – as well as other women who shaped Esperanto in its early years, this chapter joins the debate as to what drew ordinary people to learn and use a constructed language. The women analysed here were not exceptional scientists like Marie Skłodowska-Curie (1867–1934), trailblazing political activists such as Emmeline Pankhurst (1858–1928) or feminist pioneers like Eliza Orzeszkowa (1841–1910). Yet, the often-overlooked presence and contributions of women in Esperantujo – from attending and organising events to running clubs and publishing in the language – raise several questions. Who were these women attracted to Esperanto in the early 1900s, and what did they do with the language? What kinds of experiences did Esperanto and its community afford them that may not have been accessible elsewhere at the time? And why did women invest their time and money to travel abroad to discuss art, literature and social causes with fellow Esperanto speakers from around the world?

An analysis of the Beveridge sisters and other Esperanto-speaking women demonstrates how women used Esperanto as a means to build more egalitarian and inclusive social spaces. This occurred at a time when, in most countries, women were barred from holding office in government, denied the right to vote, and often excluded from educational spaces that remained largely segregated by gender.[3]

This chapter asks, first, what attracted so many women to Esperanto and how did they fit into this language community? We begin at the family level, with the distinctly middle-class Beveridge household, subsequently following other Scottish women who were locally active and who attended

Universal Congresses of Esperanto in Dresden (1908) and Antwerp (1911). These women – who were teachers, nurses, accountants and stenographers – sought ways to fit into a fast-changing society around 1900 in Europe. While navigating men's conservatism, women began systematically searching for their place in the job market. These Esperanto-speaking women might not have been at the forefront of feminism or the suffrage movement, but they were activists nonetheless, embracing Esperanto as a choice, a lifestyle and a serious alternative to women-exclusive spaces of activism.

In addition to offering a more egalitarian and inclusive space, Esperantujo also made room for women to stand out. This is what the second part of this chapter centres on by exploring how Esperanto-speaking women took part in literary competitions, translations, performing theatre plays and publishing scientific papers in the language, using Esperanto as a platform to adapt to changing times and excel.

Finding their place in Esperantujo

Between 1900 and 1913, John Beveridge and Alice Alexandra Henderson led a busy life with their three daughters and one son in Dundee, at 8 Prospect Place and, later, at 9 Magdalen Yard Road. From both addresses, it would have been a short walk down to the docks, where one could watch whaling ships coming and going, or see steamships arriving with raw jute from Bengal. At the time, Dundee was known as a 'women's town', with women making up a significant portion of the industrial workforce: around 80 per cent of working women in the city were employed in the manufacturing sector, primarily in the jute mills.[4]

The Beveridge sisters would never spend their days in jute mills, warehouses or factories surrounded by the noise of steam-driven spindles softening raw jute fibres, nor did they live the lives of working-class women in overcrowded houses with poor sanitary conditions.[5] The eldest daughter, Heather Beveridge (1886–1940), was born on 27 December 1886 in Stow, Scotland.[6] After the family moved to Dundee in 1900, she entered University College in Dundee – then part of the University of St Andrews – at the age of sixteen.[7] Upon graduating with a degree in chemistry, she was appointed as a Carnegie Research Scholar and began pursuing an academic career. In 1911, John Beveridge's and Alice Alexandra Henderson's second daughter, Lois Beveridge (1889–1946), was recorded as a twenty-two-year-old teacher living in the family's ten-room house at 9 Magdalen Yard Road, near the River Tay, on the edge of a park.[8]

In a brief biographical account written in English following the death of John Beveridge in 1943, the youngest daughter, Elizabeth Beveridge, paints a picture of the distinctly middle-class, international atmosphere she and her siblings grew up in:[9]

> Norwegian delegates to conferences in this country were frequently our guests, while pastors, teachers and professors visiting Scotland came as a matter of course to visit and consult him. Their daughters, too, used to spend some days or weeks in our home while acquiring proficiency in English [. . .] there were many others coming and going, so many that my childish memories of them are vague and confused.[10]

Elizabeth Beveridge's account describes her father's library, his involvement in various organisations and his travels to Norway. With the presence of a Dutch housemaid, John Beveridge's interest in Norwegian and some family members' fluency in Esperanto, different languages were heard in their home. Elizabeth Beveridge's biographical notes about her father convey a busy life filled with different interests and activities, which spark the imagination for the diverse and far-reaching conversations that must have been floating around the family dinner table during those years in Dundee. These surely included discussions on Protestantism, the Scottish Beekeepers' Association, the Red Cross, Nordic culture and, of course, Esperanto. Based on Elizabeth Beveridge's recollection of hosting visitors, the Beveridge sisters were raised amidst stimulating intellectual and often multilingual encounters.[11] At least two of the Beveridge children, Lois and Heather, shared their father's enthusiasm for Esperanto from 1906.

The Beveridge household fits well into the prevailing social profile of the first generation of Esperanto speakers: well-educated, middle-class people with an internationalist mindset and an openness to learn more about the world. This early Esperanto community largely comprised two overlapping age groups: those born in the 1850s, such as Ludwik Zamenhof and John Beveridge, and those born in the 1880s, like Lois and Heather Beveridge, who were entering early adulthood as the language gained momentum. Notably, this first generation – which brought together these two age groups – included a significant proportion of women. While this has been acknowledged in existing scholarship, little is known about who these women were and how they navigated Esperantujo.[12] Following the Beveridge sisters and other Esperanto-speaking women in Scotland and at Universal Congresses allows us to understand how they embraced Esperanto as a tool to assert themselves and gain prominence in their endeavours.

As indicated in Chapter 2, Lois Beveridge quickly became a fixture in the local Esperanto scene. In 1908, she gained the advanced diploma of proficiency in Esperanto (*Atesto pri Kapableco*), becoming a certified language teacher and examiner for the British Esperanto Association diplomas.[13] In her capacity as a nineteen-year-old Esperanto teacher and one of the first in Scotland, Lois Beveridge most certainly taught people older than herself. She came to head an Esperanto Circle that met on Friday evenings in her father's church and, later, at Harris Academy, where she studied in her college years.[14]

Lois Beveridge's commitment as a teacher, convener of meetings and public speaker did not go unnoticed: in December 1912, for instance, the Esperanto club in the nearby city of Perth held a celebration in her honour. The celebration recognised that her Esperanto classes had enabled Perth residents to begin learning the language and encouraged them to establish their own club.[15] Not by coincidence, a year later, Lois was elected one of the four vice-presidents of the Scottish Esperanto Federation. Hers was the only name featuring a *fino* (Miss) instead of a *sro* (Mister) prefix, which indicates that she was the only female vice-president of the Federation at the time.[16]

Esperanto – the language – gave Lois Beveridge a skill that others did not have. Esperanto – the community – gave her a space to shine. However, she was not only committed to the development of Esperantujo in Scotland. Along with many other women, Lois Beveridge travelled to continental Europe to participate in the highlight of the Esperanto experience: the Universal Congress of Esperanto.

The first Universal Congress to be held in Germany took place in 1908. That summer, some 1,500 Esperanto speakers flocked to Dresden.[17] Like other cities hosting Universal Congresses, such as Antwerp in 1911 and Kraków in 1912, Dresden had a distinct reputation for the arts and culture. In the second half of the nineteenth century, new venues for arts and sciences, such as city libraries and museums, opened their doors.[18] With higher education institutions like the Dresden Academy of Fine Arts and the University of Technology, Dresden was a city of well-educated middle classes, civil servants, merchants and bankers. The capital of Saxony was well worth a visit in its own right, and the local organisers of Universal Congresses of Esperanto followed an agenda of displaying the cultural and historical highlights of their home city to visitors.[19]

Leaving Dundee and travelling to Dresden, mingling with Esperanto speakers of a similar age from various countries, and chatting in Esperanto in outings on the river Elbe or at a theatre performance must have been thrilling. And Lois Beveridge was by no means the only woman from Scotland to attend such a congress: the high number of women present at Universal Congresses of Esperanto, as indicated by the list of participants from the 1908 Congress in Dresden, is striking.[20]

Three years later, a large group of Scotland-based Esperanto speakers attended the 1911 Universal Congress in Antwerp. The particularly strong cohort from Edinburgh that travelled to the Belgium congress that summer allows for a more nuanced picture of who these Esperanto-speaking women were in terms of their age and socio-professional background, as well as what attracted them to the language.

Founded in 1903, the Edinburgh Esperanto Club was one of the first in Scotland. Language classes were well attended, many members passed Esperanto proficiency exams, and regular talks and debate circles in Esperanto were held on topics ranging from Russian history and culture to the Chinese language.[21] The club also led the organisation of the 1908 Scottish Congress of Esperanto.[22]

Women played leading roles in running the Edinburgh club. In 1911, for instance, the club elected six of its members to serve as delegate councillors to the British Esperanto Association – four of whom were women: Isabella Mears, Miss Annie Robb, Miss A. B. Mackenzie and Miss I. E. McIntosh.[23] Such patterns suggest that Lois Beveridge was by no means a singular case. Many other young women – identified by the title 'Miss' in the announcement – took on key administrative positions, just as Lois Beveridge did as vice-president of the Federation.[24] Similarly, it was a woman – Jane Baird – who was the first author of the bilingual (English–Esperanto, Esperanto–English) *Edinburgh Esperanto Pocket Dictionary*, which was first published in 1915 and became so popular that it saw frequent new editions until 1939.[25]

Going beyond the local club in Edinburgh, a total of sixty-five women departed from Scotland to participate in the Universal Congress of Esperanto in Antwerp. With only a month until the congress, *The British Esperantist* announced that there were no more beds for ladies onboard the Gibson steamer for the journey from the port of Leith (near Edinburgh) to Antwerp.[26] By offering opportunities such as joining this cruise ship crossing, Esperanto provided these women with a framework through which they could take on leadership positions and travel independently across borders, without being accompanied by relatives, husbands or chaperones – which was uncommon for women in Europe at the time. However, more significantly, these efforts to break free from traditional roles and subordination to family affairs is closely related to the then emerging ideal of the 'new woman' – a figure increasingly associated with independence, education, mobility and engagement in public life.[27]

The new woman: nurses, teachers and stenographers in search of inclusiveness

Following the trips of these Scottish women to Universal Congresses in Dresden, Antwerp and Kraków enables an understanding of how these women fit into – or not – wider society at the time. Twenty-two of the sixty-five Scottish women (33 per cent) who attended the 1911 Universal Congress of Esperanto were listed in the attendance records as professionals, compared to twenty-one out of the forty-one men (51 per cent). While men were listed more frequently as actuaries, bankers, lawyers, city clerks, accountants, solicitors and engineers, eight women were listed as teachers, five as stenographers, three as accountants, three as nurses, and one each as typewriter, cashier and journalist.[28]

These figures show that most women who engaged with Esperanto worked in socially reproductive jobs such as nursing or teaching.[29] Meanwhile, many others worked in what were at the time 'modern' office jobs, engaging on a daily basis with cutting-edge communication technologies like stenotypes and typewriters. Compared to their mothers, these modern women were from a different generation: they were educated and skilled in new fields, they were independent and earned a living in salaried positions.[30] In their professional lives, these women were performing increasingly vital office management work, including time management, bookkeeping and internal communications. In the first two decades of the twentieth century, typists, secretaries, accountants and stenographers became emblematic professions, generally occupied by women.[31] Such professions represented the rapid structural shifts in society and economy, as well as the growth of the tertiary sector.[32] A young generation of women was coming into these occupations that were increasingly essential to the modern world, not without facing resistance or hesitation from their male counterparts.[33]

In the early twentieth century, Esperanto – a communication technology as modern as stenotypes and typewriters – aroused the curiosity of some of these modern women. Conversely, the skills and experiences of the 'new woman' in clerical work, in organising, recording and running meetings met the needs of an increasingly institutionalised Esperanto community.[34]

In addition, photographs from local Esperanto clubs and international congresses – as shown in Chapter 2 – showcase how Esperantujo featured a mix of gender and age groups, with children and teenagers mingling with middle-aged adults, as well as women and men side by side in clubs and congresses. These photographs, as well as these congresses' attendance records and programmes, highlight the salient presence of women in their twenties and thirties. Some of them were married and embraced Esperanto as a family affair; most were unmarried, attending these gatherings on their own; and many of them worked in modern office jobs.

Lois and Heather Beveridge belonged to this emerging generation. Respectively a teacher and an aspiring scientist, both were born in the 1880s and came of age in the era of what was referred to in the 1900s as the 'new woman'. Their lives and careers were markedly different from their mother's – who most likely spent her life caring for her children and assisting her husband in his parish duties.[35] By contrast, Lois and Heather Beveridge were part of a generation of women who strove to join the workforce, many of whom delved into professions that did not exist a generation earlier. Moreover, they were partly shaped by a broader demographic trend in early twentieth-century Britain, which was marked by a significant surplus of women in relation to men in the overall population.[36] Quite a few of these women remained unmarried, but gained a degree of independence by taking up salaried positions – which marked a shift in the social and economic roles available to women at the time.[37]

The history of these women has frequently been written from the perspective of political activism – as a history of either law-breaking militancy or of social reformism.[38] On the more radical side, feminists like Emmeline Pankhurst led the struggle for women's rights by demanding structural changes in society, even endorsing violence when deemed necessary.[39] Many others – including numerous female schoolteachers nurturing young minds and employed by the state – actively engaged in the cause for women's suffrage, participating in demonstrations and occasionally smashing windows during demonstrations.[40] However, also among women themselves, debates persisted over how far the fight for women's rights should go and what forms activism ought to take.[41]

By contrast, the perspective of social reformism drew on the lens of women-only organisations – which included, for instance, the International Council of Women (ICW), founded in the US in 1888, and the National Union of Women Workers (NUWW), founded in Britain in 1895. Among the key figures of such women-only organisations were Louisa Hubbard (1836–1906), Louise Creighton (1850–1936) and the marchioness Ishbel of Aberdeen and Temair (1857–1939). Nearly all these women – who advocated for women's rights through doing philanthropic work and pressuring politicians to pass bills – came from affluent backgrounds, which consolidated the highest ranks of these organisations as spaces for wealthy women.[42]

Esperanto emerged alongside a number of women-only organisations. The ICW was founded at the time when Ludwik Zamenhof published Esperanto's first textbook. The German Women's International League for Peace and Freedom was founded in 1904, a year before the first international Esperanto congress in 1905. Even though, at first glance, ICW's commitment to neutrality and this organisation's strong links with Protestantism could have made it appealing to Esperanto-speaking women like Lois and Heather Beveridge, this does not seem to have been the case. After all, leadership roles in these women-only organisations were reserved for older women – thus from a different generation – and, above all, women from a different social background. The ICW led by Ishbel of Aberdeen and Temair, for instance, drew an elite social composition that was de facto, if not explicitly, closed to middle-class women such as the Esperanto-speaking women from Dundee and Edinburgh described above. Ultimately, the Beveridge sisters found in Esperantujo a more inclusive space to express themselves, gain freedom from the societal roles expected from them and take on leading roles in their local engagements with a global cause, making Esperanto a means of activism.

While the suffragettes tended to be more open to confrontational forms of activism, women-only organisations had a more elitist composition and spoke to the interests of a generation and class that did not necessarily relate to the needs of the 'new woman'. Alongside these straightforward forms of activism, Esperanto also emerged as a means for activism: one that did not advance women's rights per se but aided in the pursuit of more egalitarian and inclusive communication spaces. Most importantly, Esperanto became the basis to foster gender-inclusive spaces that, unlike the previously mentioned movements and organisations, were not women-only.

While the emergence of modern office jobs and the demographic surplus of women in places like Britain offered young women new opportunities to express different aspirations and take on roles beyond those of wife and mother, they continued to face widespread discrimination. Their access to the job market remained hierarchical and precarious, and several informal spaces for leisure and sociability continued to be similarly restrictive. Against this backdrop, Esperantujo provided women with a space of relative egalitarianism and inclusion – one that they struggled to find elsewhere in society.

Esperanto was by no means the only resource through which they could achieve this – see, for instance, how tennis clubs and other sports spaces at the time also took a relatively inclusive approach to gender.[43] Yet Esperanto was the entryway these specific women and numerous others chose in order to experiment with more egalitarian relations in which men, women and people from different social classes and age groups featured side by side. Through Esperanto, these women carved a more egalitarian microcosm in a society that they otherwise perceived as exclusionary and discriminatory.

Closed universities, open books: writing, starring and producing knowledge in Esperantoland

When Lois Beveridge arrived in Dresden, she would have met many young Esperanto speakers who had also travelled long distances. The congress reports from 1908 mention young attendees from places such as Sweden and France, also explicitly underscoring the many young women who travelled from Britain – not without a wry side note remarking: 'that these proud young British women would bring themselves to speaking in a different language abroad other than their own idiom, I would not have deemed possible.'[44]

Dresden itself had a vibrant Esperanto scene at the time. In 1910, the city was home to sixteen Esperanto clubs. At least one of them – the Damenverein (Ladies' Club) – was exclusively for women. Some concentrated

Figure 3.1: Some participants of the Universal Congress who travelled from Scotland to Kraków in 1912 (no. 143 in the picture is Jane Baird; no. 144 is John Beveridge). Source: Julius Glück, *Jubilea Universala Kongreso Esperantista: Albumo Kraków 1912* (Kraków: Ludowa, 1912), 63. Courtesy of the University of St Andrews Libraries and Museums, PM8201.C6

on a certain socio-professional profile, including Esperanto clubs for academics and for police officers, which may have been male-dominated. Yet the high number of female members in the numerous local clubs is noticeable: out of the 547 registered Esperanto speakers in Dresden, 198 (37 per cent) were women. Eighty of these were listed as 'Fräulein', indicating young and/or unmarried women.[45]

Yet Dresden – or Dundee and Edinburgh for that matter – only epitomises a much broader picture. Numerous images of Esperanto meetings at this time – be they club gatherings in Perth, the Universal Congress of Esperanto in Kraków (see Figure 3.1) or the 1911 Brazilian Congress of Esperanto in Juiz de Fora (see Figure 3.2) – confirm the same pattern: a high number of Esperanto-speaking women, many of whom were in their twenties and thirties.

While women played leading roles in the day-to-day running of local clubs, many stood out in the cultural programmes of national and

Figure 3.2: Group photography at the Fourth Brazilian Congress of Esperanto, in Juiz de Fora, 1911. Courtesy of the Department of Planned Languages, Austrian National Library, ID: Alma466702

international Esperanto congresses. In Dresden, for instance, the German actress Hedwig Reicher (1884–1971) took the lead part in the Esperanto rendition of Johann Wolfgang von Goethe's *Iphigenie*, performed at the Dresden Opera. Similarly, a group of young Swedish women took centre stage in August Strindberg's theatre play *Miss Julie* in Esperanto.[46] While professional singers or actresses such as Hedwig Reicher were invited to perform at congresses and learned the basics of the language for the occasion, most of these performers were ordinary Esperanto speakers and, thus, amateur artists.

This was also the case at the 1912 Universal Congress in Kraków, when performers from the Lviv Opera House staged the Esperanto rendition of Stanisław Moniuszko's *Halka*, the most emblematic Polish opera of the nineteenth century.[47] These events afforded performers access to a large audience, with the combination of emblematic national works – from *Iphigenie* and *Miss Julie* to *Halka* – and an international language empowering women to stand out on the big stage.

However, women did not only perform. They actively contributed to the growing corpus of Esperanto literature through poetry, novels and theatre plays. Mary Jane Hare, for instance, a Dundee resident, wrote an original three-act comedy for the Sixth Scottish Congress of Esperanto in Dundee, in 1911. Titled *The Foreign Correspondent*, it was featured multiple times in local newspapers and Esperanto newsletters. Similarly, women gave talks at Esperanto congresses, discussing topics ranging from missionary work to the potential of Esperanto in the Red Cross.[48]

With the Universal Congresses becoming a fixture in Esperantujo, literary events and competitions soon became an integral part of it. Here another key figure, already mentioned in Chapter 2, rose to prominence: Marie Hankel (1844–1929). Hankel founded the Esperantista Literatura Asocio (Esperanto Literature Association) during the 1911 Universal Congress in Antwerp and served as this association's first president – and who, for these and other reasons, deserves more detailed attention.[49]

Unlike the much younger Beveridge sisters and their 'new woman' generation, Marie Hankel – born in 1844 in Schwerin, northern Germany – only became interested in Esperanto in her early sixties. Her husband, the well-known mathematician Hermann Hankel, had passed away prematurely at the age of thirty-four in 1873. In 1905, Marie Hankel moved to Dresden.[50] In addition to teaching the language and founding an Esperanto club in 1906, she co-organised several Esperanto gatherings in Dresden and became one of the co-organisers of the 1908 Universal Congress.[51] Not only did Marie Hankel attend all the Universal Congresses of Esperanto held in Europe between 1905 and 1913, she also attended the Universal Congress in Washington DC in 1910, the first one outside Europe.[52] By that time, she had started publishing in Esperanto on a number of topics, from theatre to architecture and literature, while also publishing her own poetry in prestigious periodicals such as *La Revuo*.[53]

Women like Marie Hankel did not dominate the pages of *La Revuo* but, among still predominantly male authors, they stood out as female writers.[54] While several Esperanto magazines at the time were dedicated to world news and Esperanto-related updates, *La Revuo* centred on literature, and thus became the leading outlet for the development of an Esperanto canon of translations and original texts. Ludwik Zamenhof himself was a driving force behind *La Revuo* and, in the same magazine issue that featured one of Hankel's poems in 1908, Zamenhof contributed a translation that opened with the following lines:

> La vivo de virino estas eterne brulanta flamo de amo, diras unuj. La vivo de virino estas sinoferado, certigas aliaj. La vivo de virino estas patrineco, krias parto da homoj. La vivo de virino estas amuziĝado, ŝercas aliaj. La virto de virino estas blinda kredo, ĥore konsentas ĉiuj. La virinoj kredas blinde; ili amas, sin oferas, edukas infanojn [. . .], kaj tamen la mondo ial rigardis ilin senkonfide, kaj de tempo al tempo ĝi esprimas sian opinion en formo de riproĉo aŭ averto: vi ne estas en ordo![55]

These lines – which characterise the contributions of women as limited to their societal roles as mothers, carers and faithful companions – are the opening sentences of the novel *Marta*, by Eliza Orzeszkowa (1841–1910). At the heart of the novel, first published in Polish in 1873, is the life and hardship of Marta Świcka. Widowed at a young age, the single mother to a young daughter, she desperately seeks to make ends meet with the skills she has: some education, basic French, household skills and sewing. Yet, wherever Marta tries to find a job, she is outperformed, often by men, other skilled women or cheaper foreign workers.[56]

Other translations by Ludwik Zamenhof – from Shakespeare's works to the Old Testament – may be better known, yet here in *La Revuo* was the Esperanto version of the work of one of the best-known Polish novelists, social reformers and literary voices for women's rights.[57] Eliza Orzeszkowa was an early strong voice of women's emancipation, yet a voice in Polish that was largely hidden behind a language barrier for women from other national and linguistic backgrounds. With her literary work, Eliza Orzeszkowa set the tone and the themes for women's rights well before Emmeline Pankhurst (1858–1928) in Britain or Charlotte Perkins Gilman (1860–1935) in the US – women who spoke and wrote in English and often took the limelight as the trailblazers of the first generation of activists for women's emancipation.[58] Through Esperanto, a feminist icon became better known beyond Polish-language circles – an icon that was later nominated for the Nobel Prize in Literature in 1905 and 1909.

By contrast, Marie Hankel was never nominated for the Nobel Prize. However, in 1909, at the Fifth Universal Congress in Barcelona, she won the first prize at the first poetry competition ever held at a Universal Congress for her poem *La Simbolo de l'Amo* (The Symbol of Love). Later, during her stint as president of the Esperantista Literatura Asocio, her collection of short stories and poems was published as *Sableroj* (Grains of Sand).[59]

With these publications, key controversial topics of the time – such as women's rights – gained ground in the agenda of Esperanto speakers. Adding to these debates, in the 1910 Universal Congress of Esperanto in Washington DC, Marie Hankel gave a speech on women's rights and universal suffrage, asserting that 'universities may be closed to women, but thank goodness books are open'.[60] Her speech defended women's rights not by adopting 'noisy and violent' acts of protest, but by insistently seeking ways to make women's voices heard and respected. Her speech was later translated into English and featured in *The Washington Herald*, thus reaching a far wider non-Esperanto-speaking public.[61]

Hankel's words in Washington DC hint as to why so many women found their ways in and through Esperanto. In a world structured around gender inequality, spaces dedicated to creativity and the arts allowed women to express themselves. There were gender barriers in higher education and social barriers in women-only organisations. However, despite all, women were finally making it into the lists of Nobel Prize nominees, and the first woman to actually win a Nobel Prize was not far from the Esperanto scene: Marie Skłodowska-Curie (1867–1934).

The career of Marie Skłodowska-Curie was one achieved against many odds in terms of gender and social – as well as linguistic – barriers. Working in French academia meant, after all, developing a career in a language that was not her first. She published her research primarily in French and

English, at a time when English was not (yet) consolidated as the de facto global language of science. Curiously, Esperanto was on the radar of the Skłodowski family. Marie Skłodowska-Curie's elder brother, Józef Skłodowski (1863–1937) – who worked as an internist in Warsaw – took up Esperanto along with many other physicians from Warsaw. With some of these physicians, he travelled to the Universal Congress of Esperanto in Dresden in 1908. It was the Dresden congress that substantiated the appeal of Esperanto to scientists, after a number of physicians gathered and founded the Tutmonda Esperanta Kuracista Asocio (Worldwide Esperanto Medical Association, TEKA). TEKA developed into a truly transnational medical association, launching its own journals and gathering over 600 members in around 100 cities worldwide in the following years.[62]

At a time when scientific publishing was dominated by a triad of French, English and German – with some Russian interspersed – a number of leading scientists were attracted to the idea of Esperanto as a language for science.[63] This included Odo Bujwid (1857–1942), a Polish bacteriologist who had studied in Berlin and Paris and, in the process, had to master various languages including German, French and English.[64] Bujwid was part of the organising committee of the 1912 Universal Congress in Kraków, during which he also became a member of TEKA and later served as its president. His wife, Kazimiera Bujwidowa (1867–1932), was a leading figure in the women's movement then, in the generation after Eliza Orzeszkowa. While learning Esperanto for the 1912 Universal Congress, Kazimiera Bujwidowa also published her works on women's rights in Polish.[65]

Among the leading scientists attracted to Esperanto as a solution for the barriers to international communication was the German chemist Wilhelm Ostwald (1853–1935). A vocal advocate for Esperanto as a language for the sciences, Ostwald was awarded the Nobel Prize in Chemistry in 1909 – two years before Marie Skłodowska-Curie would receive her second Nobel, in 1911. By then, there were a number of scientific journals in Esperanto, publishing medical articles as well as knowledge from fields ranging from mathematics and astronomy to music. The most successful publication in this regard was the *Internacia Scienca Revuo* (International Science Review), founded in 1904.

The January 1908 issue of this journal featured a scientific article titled *Hidro de para-toluidino* (Paratoluidine hydrate).[66] The author of this chemistry paper – which analysed water loss and weight calculations – was Heather Beveridge. By the time she published her paper – a translation of an earlier version in English also authored by her – she held a degree in chemistry from the University of St Andrews and worked at the University of Edinburgh, where she co-authored a number of journal articles with the chemist James Walker.

Getting scientific papers published is not an easy undertaking – particularly as a female scientist around 1910. Heather Beveridge may never have been nominated for the Nobel Prize, but publishing in Esperanto gave international visibility to her work. According to the *Dundee Courier* – which took notice of her scientific endeavour – the young and aspiring Carnegie Research Scholar hoped that, by publishing in Esperanto, her work would be read by scholars around the world.[67] Perhaps a paper in Esperanto would not make her research widely read in mainstream academic settings. However, in Esperantujo, her contributions established her career as a leading chemist, enabling her to stand out in this more egalitarian and inclusive setting that Heather Beveridge and other women forged through the use of Esperanto.

Concluding remarks

Women were drawn to Esperanto in large numbers around 1900 – and they were crucial in making this language community thrive. They led clubs, took meeting minutes, managed club membership and finance and attended congresses abroad. But they did far more than that: they sang, performed, translated literary works, organised literary competitions, debated women's rights and published scientific articles in Esperanto. In many ways, women were an integral part of Esperantujo and, given how much time, enthusiasm, creativity and financial means they invested, Esperanto must have been an integral part of these women's lives.

In the pre-1914 years, Esperanto provided settings in which older women from the mid-century generation met younger ones who, like the Beveridge sisters, were educated, skilled, salaried and independent. This latter generation came of age when women fought for emancipation and equal rights. Many of these women who challenged their pre-assigned societal roles of mothers, carers and wives took the route of confrontational political action, whereas others joined women-only organisations or broke into the male-dominated spaces of science and literature by being nominated to and winning Nobel Prizes.

At first glance, Esperanto may seem to only marginally fit this broader landscape of early twentieth-century political activism and scientific development. After all, in the long term, Esperanto became neither the currency of scientific knowledge production nor the ideal language for political activism and social reform. The latter were more effectively pursued through demonstrations and pamphlets in vernacular languages, targeted at local and national publics, as done by Kazimiera Bujwidowa or Emmeline Pankhurst. However, Esperanto did find its place in this scenario. Unlike women-only spaces of activism and male-dominated spaces of scientific knowledge production, local Esperanto clubs and Universal Congresses emerged as progressive spaces. As a consequence of women's efforts in the early decades of the language, using Esperanto came to imply forging largely egalitarian spaces in an otherwise unequal society, where speaking and writing in Esperanto meant placing oneself in a common ground where men and women, as well as younger and older people, met on more equal terms. Perhaps surprisingly, a language designed to encourage cross-border communication and the bridging of national and linguistic backgrounds also became mobilised as a means to establish an alternative space, in which Esperanto speakers also bridged gender divides.

Notes

1 Wendy Heller, *Lidia: The Life of Lidia Zamenhof, the Daughter of Esperanto* (Oxford: Georg Ronald, 1985).

2 Mark Fettes, 'The Lady, the Linguists, and the International Language', *Language Problems and Language Planning* 25, no. 2 (2001): 177–84.

3 Voting exceptions were rare, such as Denmark, where women were allowed to vote in local elections from 1908, and in the Grand Duchy of Finland – then part of the Russian Empire – where women were granted the right to vote and stand for Parliament from 1905. See Karen Hunt, 'Suffrage Internationalism in Practice: Dora Montefiore and the Lessons of Finnish Women's Enfranchisement', in Alexandra Hughes-Johnson and Lyndsey Jenkins, eds. *The Politics of Women's Suffrage: Local, National and International Dimensions* (London: University of London Press, 2021), 286–7.

4 This compared to less than 30 per cent in Edinburgh or in Aberdeen at the time; see Graham R. Smith, *'The Making of a Woman's Town': Household and Gender in Dundee, 1890–1940* (PhD thesis, University of Stirling, 1996).

5 Jim Tomlinson, *Dundee and the Empire: 'Juteopolis' 1850–1939* (Edinburgh: Edinburgh University Press, 2014); Bruce Lenman, Charlotte Lythe and Enid Gauldie, *Dundee and Its Textile Industry, 1850–1914* (Dundee: Abertay Historical Society, 1969); Enid Gauldie, 'The Dundee Jute Industry', in *Scottish Textile History*, ed. John Butt and Kenneth Ponting (Aberdeen: Aberdeen University Press, 1987), 112–25.

6 Brief research about Heather Beveridge's life and career as a chemist has been undertaken by Marelene Rayner-Canham and Geoffrey Rayner-Canham in *Chemistry Was Their Life: Pioneering British Women Chemists, 1880–1949* (London: Imperial College Press, 2008), 276–7.

7 On Dundee and the founding of the University College, see Murdo Macdonald, 'The Patron, the Professor and the Painter: Cultural Activity in Dundee at the Close of the Nineteenth Century,' in *Victorian Dundee: Image and Realities*, ed. Christopher A. Whatley and Bob Harris (East Linton: Tuckwell Press, 2000), 199–200.

8 Scotland Census, 1911, National Records of Scotland, Ref: 282/18/5, '1911, Beveridge, John'.

9 K. Theodore Hoppen, *The Mid-Victorian Generation, 1846–1886* (London: Clarendon Press, 1998), 334–44.

10 John Beveridge Collection, Ms36244/15.

11 John Beveridge Collection, Ms36244/15, 5.

12 Garvía, *Esperanto and Its Rivals*, 95–8; Forster, *The Esperanto Movement*, 268–99.

13 'Local Esperanto Successes', *The Dundee Courier*, 11 October 1907.

14 The first classes were held in 1908, and those at Harris Academy began in 1911. See 'Dundee: Kvaronjara Raporto', *The British Esperantist*, April 1911, 78.

15 See *The Perthshire Advertiser*, 21 December 1912.

16 John Beveridge Collection, Ms38908/16.

17 *Kvara Universala Kongreso de Esperanto* (Paris: Esperantista Centra Oficejo, 1909).

18 The Dresden Museum of Ethnology was founded in 1875, a new opera house opened in the 1870s, the Dresden City Museum was founded in 1891 and the City Library opened in 1900.

19 'Esperanto Reaches Its Semi-Jubilee', *Dundee Courier*, 4 June 1912.

20 *Kvara Universala Kongreso de Esperanto.*

21 See, for instance, *The British Esperantist*, February 1908, 39; *The British Esperantist*, March 1908, 45; *The British Esperantist*, April 1908, 76.

22 See John Beveridge Collection, Ms38908/13.

23 See 'B.E.A. Delegate Councillors', *The British Esperantist*, April 1911, 79.

24 See *The British Esperantist*, May, 1911, 98.

25 Jane Baird, William Harvey and John Mabon Warden, *The Edinburgh Esperanto Pocket Dictionary* (Edinburgh: Thomas Nelson and Sons, 1915). See also 'Bibliografio', *Belga Esperantisto*, October, 1931, 110.

26 See 'Skotaj karavanoj al Antverpeno', *The British Esperantist*, June 1911, 117; 'Karavanoj al Antverpeno', *The British Esperantist*, July 1911, 138.

27 Estelle B. Freedman, 'The New Woman: Changing Views of Women in the 1920s', *The Journal of American History* 61, no. 2 (1974): 372–93; Sally Ledger, *The New Woman: Fiction and Feminism at the Fin de Siècle* (Manchester: Manchester University Press, 1997).

28 See *Sepa Universala Kongreso de Esperanto* (Paris: Esperantista Centra Oficejo, 1912), 125–7. This statement refers to those participants who are listed with a profession next to their name.

29 This socio-professional picture, however, was more varied, including professions such as dressmaker. See Scotland Census, 1911, National Records of Scotland, Ref: 685/2 44/ 20, '1911 Simpson, Lucy May'.

30 Delphine Gardey, 'Mechanizing Writing and Photographing the Word: Utopias, Office Work, and Histories of Gender and Technology', *History and Technology* 17, no. 4 (2001): 319–52, here 320.

31 Sharon Hartman Strom, *Beyond the Typewriter: Gender, Class, and the Origins of Modern American Office Work, 1900–1930* (Urbana: University of Illinois Press, 1992), 5–6.

32 Delphine Gardey, 'The Standardization of a Technical Practice: Typing (1883–1930)', *History and Technology* 15, no. 4 (1999): 313–43; Strom, *Beyond the Typewriter*, 17–18.

33 Ken Shackleton, 'Gender Segregation in Scottish Chartered Accountancy: The Deployment of Male Concerns about the Admission of Women, 1900–25', *Accounting, Business & Financial History* 9, no. 1 (1999): 135–56.

34 Kim England and Kate Boyer, 'Women's Work: The Feminization and Shifting Meanings of Clerical Work', *Journal of Social History* 43, no. 2 (2009): 307–40, here 310–11; Graham Lowe, *Women in the Administrative Revolution: The Feminization of Clerical Work* (Toronto: University of Toronto Press, 1987); Angel Kwolek-Folland, *Engendering Business: Men and Women in the Corporate Office, 1870–1930* (Baltimore, MD: Johns Hopkins University Press, 1994).

35 The generational difference between mother and daughters, as well as the expectations around a mid-Victorian, middle-class wife and mother, may explain the silence around Alice Alexandra Henderson in the otherwise rich archive of John Beveridge. See, for instance, Patricia Branca, *Silent Sisterhood: Middle-Class Women in the Victorian Home* (London: Routledge, 2012); Elizabeth Langland, *Nobody's Angels: Middle-Class Women and Domestic Ideology in Victorian Culture* (Ithaca, NY: Cornell University Press, 1995).

36 Pat Thane, '"Well-Bred and Conventional Ladies": The National Council of Women of Great Britain and Ireland/Northern Ireland', *Women's History Review* 32, no. 2 (2023): 172–89, here 172.

37 On this generation and their novel career paths, see Arlene Young, *From Spinster to Career Woman: Middle-Class Women and Work in Victorian England* (Montreal: McGill-Queen's Press, 2019).

38 See, for instance, Lucy Delap, *The Feminist Avant-Garde: Transatlantic Encounters of the Early Twentieth Century* (Cambridge: Cambridge University

Press, 2009); Lucy Delap, *Feminisms: A Global History* (Chicago: University of Chicago Press, 2020); Susan Ware, *Why They Marched: Untold Stories of the Women Who Fought for the Right to Vote* (Cambridge, MA: Belknap Press, 2019).

39 Paula Bartley, *Emmeline Pankhurst* (London: Routledge, 2002), 44–67, 96–115; June Purvis, 'Emmeline Pankhurst (1858–1928), Suffragette Leader and Single Parent in Edwardian Britain', *Women's History Review* 20, no. 1 (2011): 87–108.

40 Alison Oram, *Women Teachers and Feminist Politics, 1900–39* (Manchester: Manchester University Press, 1996), 21–4.

41 Thane, 'Well-Bred and Conventional Ladies', 173–5.

42 See Leila J. Rupp, *Worlds of Women: The Making of an International Women's Movement* (Princeton: Princeton University Press, 1997); Ann Taylor Allen and Anne Cova, 'Introduction: Transnational Women's Activism', *Women's History Review* 32, no. 2 (2023): 165–71, here 167–8.

43 Robert Lake, 'Gender and Etiquette in British Lawn Tennis 1870–1939: A Case Study of "Mixed Doubles"', *The International Journal of the History of Sport* 29, no. 5 (2012): 691–710.

44 As stated in the anonymous congress report in the original: 'Dass die stolzen Britinnen sich herablassen würden, im Auslande in einer anderen Sprache als ihrem heimischen Idiom zu reden, hätte ich nie für möglich gehalten.' Sächsisches Esperanto-Institut Dresden, ed., *Bericht* (Dresden: Druckerei des Esperanto-Verlages F. Emil Boden, 1908), 43–4.

45 *Gesellschaft Esperanto Dresden* (Dresden: Gebr. Arnhold, 1910).

46 Sächsisches Esperanto-Institut Dresden, ed., *Bericht*, 52–3. See Johann Wolfgang von Goethe, *Ifigenio en Taŭrido: Dramo en kvin aktoj*, trans. Ludwik Zamenhof (Paris: Hachette, 1908).

47 Julius Glück, *La Jubilea Kongreso de Esperanto 1912: Rememoraĵoj kaj oficialaj dokumentokoj* (Purmerend: J. Muusses, 1912), 25–6. On *Halka* and the Lviv Opera House, see Philipp Ther, *Centre Stage: Operatic Culture and Nation Building in Nineteenth-Century Central Europe* (West Lafayette, IN: Purdue University Press, 2014), 111–32.

48 John Beveridge Collection, Ms38908/15.

49 Geoffrey Sutton, *Concise Encyclopedia of the Original Literature of Esperanto, 1887–2007* (New York: Mondial, 2008), 52–3.

50 See, for instance, *Gesellschaft Esperanto Dresden* (Dresden: Gebr. Arnhold, 1910).

51 See Bernhard Pabst, *Marie Hankel (1844–1929): Esperanto-Dichterin, Organisatorin, Feministin* (Bonn: Selbstverlag, 2002), 5.

52 See 'Parolo pri virinrajtoj', *Amerika Esperantisto*, October 1910, 66.

53 For instance, Marie Hankel, 'La batalo pro la vivo', *La Revuo*, III, 1908, 412.

54 See Javier Alcalde, 'Pioneers of Internationalism: Esperanto and the First World War', in *Multilingual Environments in the Great War*, ed. Julian Walker and Christophe Declercq (London: Bloomsbury, 2021), 44–57, here 48.

55 'The life of a woman is an eternally burning flame of love, some say. A woman's life is self-sacrifice, others affirm. A woman's life is motherhood, some people vociferate. A woman's life is entertaining, others joke. The virtue of a woman is blind faith, everyone agrees. Women believe blindly; they love, sacrifice themselves, raise children [. . .] and yet, for some reason, the world looks at them with distrust, and from time to time they express their opinion in the form of a reprimand or a warning: You are not ok!' 'Marta. Rakonto de Eliza Orzeszko (el la pola lingvo, kun permeso de la aŭtorino, tradukis Dro L. L. Zamenhof)', *La Revuo*, III, 1908, 49.

56 Eliza Orzeszkowa, *Marta* (Warsaw: S. Lewentala, 1885).

57 On the women's question, see Eliza Orzeszkowa, *Kilka słów o kobietach* (Lviv: Rogosz, 1873); see also Barbara Noworolska, *Eliza Orzeszkowa. Trwanie, pamięć, historia* (Białystok: Wydawnictwo Uniwersytetu w Białymstoku, 2005).

58 See, for instance, Delap, *Feminisms*, 31–6; Ware, *Why They Marched*, 4–8, 64–73.

59 Pabst, *Marie Hankel*, 8; Marie Hankel, 'La Simbolo de l'Amo', *La Revuo*, III, 1909, 92; Marie Hankel, *Sableroj* (Leipzig: Deutsche Esperanto Buchhandlung, 1911).

60 *Libro de la Sesa Internacia Kongreso* (Washington DC: La Kongreso, 1910).

61 'Woman in Esperanto Asks Equal Rights', *The Washington Herald*, 21 August, 1910, 2.

62 Marcel Koschek, 'TEKA: A Transnational Network of Esperanto-Speaking Physicians', *Hungarian Historical Review* 10, no. 2 (2021): 243–66.

63 See Gordin, *Scientific Babel*, 1–22, 105–30; Bernhard Struck, '(Plan)Sprachen und Wissen (-sordnungen) um 1900', in *Wissen Ordnen und Entgrenzen – Vom Analogen Zum Digitalen Europa?*, ed. Joachim Berger and Thorsten Wübbena (Göttingen: Vandenhoeck & Ruprecht, 2023), 27–46.

64 Katharina Kreuder-Sonnen, 'From Transnationalism to Olympic Internationalism: Polish Medical Experts and International Scientific Exchange, 1885–1939', *Contemporary European History* 25, no. 2 (2016): 207–31.

65 See Kazimiera Bujwidowa, *Kwestya kobieca: czy kobieta powinna mieć te same prawa co mężczyzna?* (Kraków: nakł. Towarzystwo Wydawniczego 'Encyklopedyi Ludowej', 1909). See also Zuzanna Kołodziejska-Smagała, 'Polish-Jewish Female Writers and the Women's Emancipation Movements in the Late Nineteenth and Early Twentieth Centuries', *Aspasia* 16 (2022): 110–29.

66 Heather Beveridge, 'Hidro de para-toluidino', *Internacia Science Revuo* 5 (1908), 7–11.

67 *Dundee Courier*, 16 January, 1908.

Chapter 4

Speaking of the Lord to the master: John Beveridge, Ludwik Zamenhof and the Esperanto translation of the Bible

In June 1909, William Main Page (1869–1940) – a lawyer and Presbyterian layman living in Edinburgh – sent a postcard to John Beveridge. Writing in Esperanto, Page informed that John Beveridge had been elected as a member of the Bible Translation Committee. Along with Page and a number of Christian Esperanto speakers based in Britain, Beveridge would combine his devotion to God and to then-developing Esperanto to become a leading member of the team responsible for preparing the first Esperanto translation of the New Testament.

Ludwik Zamenhof considered the translation of the Bible a priority. Such a publication would convey the message that, despite Esperanto being secular, this language community also welcomed people holding religious convictions. Additionally, a Bible in Esperanto would showcase the breadth of this constructed language, as translating this canonical text would display Esperanto's advanced vocabulary. While Zamenhof began translating the Old Testament from Hebrew in 1910, a group of Britain-based Esperanto speakers translated the New Testament from Ancient Greek, gave sermons in Esperanto at congresses and, in 1911, founded the Kristana Esperantista Ligo Internacia (International League of Christian Esperantists, KELI).

Yet, this collaborative endeavour would soon encounter a series of multilingual challenges: how to translate from Ancient Greek into Esperanto words that already caused headaches to translators of the Bible into other languages, such as παρρησία (Latinised as *parrhesia*)? What to do with χαρις (frequently translated as 'grace') if the major monolingual Esperanto dictionary at the time did not recognise the word *graco*?[1] Given issues of vocabulary development and interfaith dialogue, how could 'Elohim' and 'Jehovah' be translated in the Old Testament in a way that would not conflict with the translation of 'God' in the New Testament? Between the words of the Lord and the words of the language's *majstro* (master) – Ludwik Zamenhof – who would win the disputes around how to coin Esperanto terms for 'forgiveness', 'propitiation' and 'God' at a time when the language was still developing its vocabulary?

Considering how Bible translation has long been a milestone in European imperialism overseas, this chapter explores how the Esperanto Bible was meant as part and parcel of a language creation process.[2] This translation involved, among other languages, Russian, Polish, Hebrew, Ancient Greek and English – and, while the first generations of Esperanto speakers produced materials and translated texts, they also developed vocabulary to name things that had not been initially named by Zamenhof. Along with the ways in which meeting, translating, publishing and exchanging postcards animated Esperantujo, the Bible Translation Committee would test Esperanto's capacity for fostering an interfaith network of Jewish, Anglican, Presbyterian, Episcopal and Quaker volunteer translators who exchanged drafts by correspondence and operated in multiple languages.

This chapter reviews how multilingualism, language ideologies, vocabulary development and correspondence intertwined in the process of translating the Bible into Esperanto in the 1910s. To do so, we begin by analysing the plea of early Esperanto speakers for a translation of canonical religious texts. This is followed by a reconstruction of the history of the Bible Translation Committee, their encounters with Zamenhof and controversies over the development of faith and vocabulary. The chapter then investigates how the translation of the Bible into several languages has historically paved the way to modernity both in European and colonial settings. As the Bible became framed alternatively as an index of Western 'civilisation' and as a specimen of universality, its translations consolidated a form of modernity that made room for the globalisation of faith. The international postal services operating in Europe – and the way they were disrupted during wartime – reinsert the chapter's discussion into the transnational history of Europe, languages and international communication.

Building a corpus and a community

Ludwik Zamenhof launched the basis of Esperanto in 1887, in a booklet in Russian – the language in which he had been educated in tsarist Russia. Aside from an introduction justifying the need for an international auxiliary language, this booklet contained a grammar section, a dictionary and writing samples. Amidst original and translated poetry and prose, two writing samples stood out in this booklet. The first text published in Esperanto, on page nineteen of the Russian original of the book, was *Patro Nia* – Zamenhof's translation of the Lord's Prayer – which was followed by the initial verses of the Old Testament's book of Genesis.[3] Hence, it is no exaggeration to say that the history of Esperanto translation began with religious texts.

In the years following 1887, Ludwik Zamenhof translated scientific articles and various literary works including Charles Dickens's, William Shakespeare's, Nikolai Gogol's and Friedrich Schiller's, as well as Indian tales and Hans Christian Andersen's fables. He also translated lesser-known short stories, novels and poems with the purpose of validating the grammar rules he proposed. All of this would demonstrate the potential of Esperanto for literary use and, ultimately, for the creation of original Esperanto literature.[4]

Ludwik Zamenhof conceived himself as the initiator and enabler of the language, but not its owner. Following these initial steps and translations, Zamenhof took a back seat in the development of Esperanto, declaring the language 'property of society' and renouncing all personal rights over it.[5] In providing these specimens of translations, he set the stage for the organic development of the language, leaving the task of developing further vocabulary and a literary corpus to Esperanto's emerging language community.

Translating distinguishable literary works was a way of giving visibility to Esperanto: if the language is developed enough to express the nuances of Eliza Orzeszkowa's *Marta* or William Shakespeare's *Hamlet*, it should be developed enough to convey any complex form of human feeling and expression. This logic meant that translating religious scriptures became a priority for Zamenhof and other Esperanto pioneers:

> Neniu libro estas tiel konata en la tuta civilizita mondo, kiel la Biblio; kaj se ni povus montri al la mondo, ke Esperanto posedas la tradukon de la tuta Biblio, tio estus por ni tre potenca propagandilo. [. . .]

> Por la plimulto de la nuntempaj kulturaj lingvoj la Biblio estis la ĉefa bazo, sur kiu la lingvoj literaturiĝis kaj disvolviĝis; tial ankaŭ por nia lingvo sendube estos tre grave, se ĝi posedos en si en plena tuteco tiun bazon kun ĝiaj multaj vortoj kaj esprimoj, kiuj fariĝis elementa necesaĵo por ĉiu nuntempa kultura lingvo.[6]

Drawing on his Jewish origins, Ludwik Zamenhof largely took this effort into his own hands in 1906 by translating excerpts from Ecclesiastes – the Old Testament's first book in the canonical order – from Hebrew into Esperanto.[7] Encouraged by the interest shown by Esperanto speakers – many of whom inquired about the translation during the 1907 Universal Congress of Esperanto, held in Cambridge – Zamenhof continued translating the initial books of the Old Testament over the following years. He initially published these translations in the monthly periodical *La Revuo*, later reissuing them as standalone volumes with the French publishing house Hachette.[8] In the preambles to his translations, Zamenhof not only clarified some of his vocabulary choices but also expressed a degree of unease regarding this task:

> La personoj religiaj volu pardoni min, ke mi – ne pastro kaj ne specialisto en aferoj religiaj – entreprenis fari la tradukon de verko religia; sed mi povas min senkulpigi per tio, ke mi tradukis la Psalmaron ne kiel verkon religian, sed kiel gravegan verkon de la homara literaturo. Por celoj pure religiaj eble pli aŭ malpli frue aperos alia traduko, farita de ekleziuloj-specialistoj.[9]

In the preambles, Ludwik Zamenhof described his approach to the scriptures as texts of literary rather than religious value. However, while his Jewish background and knowledge of Hebrew qualified him to translate books from the Old Testament, he did not feel similarly well placed to translate the New Testament from Ancient Greek. This was one of the reasons why he chose not to undertake this endeavour on his own.

Most importantly, Ludwik Zamenhof was far from being the only Esperanto speaker concerned with the scriptures. E. Neumark from Grodno, then in tsarist Russia, translated Ruth – the eighth book of the Old Testament – into Esperanto in 1893, drawing on the original in Hebrew and on its previous translations in Russian, German, Arabic and Persian.[10] In 1906, W. B. Mielck and F. Stefan translated Matthew – the first book of the

New Testament – based not on the Ancient Greek original[11] but on Martin Luther's translation into German.[12]

Meanwhile, other Esperanto speakers published translations of scriptures in *La Revuo* and other magazines such as the Catholic periodical *Espero Katolika* (Catholic Hope) – published since 1903 – and the interdenominational, predominantly Protestant periodical *Dia Regno* (God's Kingdom) – launched in 1908. At the time, a periodical such as *Dia Regno* had a significant transnational reach, as it was subscribed to by individuals and Esperanto clubs in Germany, Finland, the US, Portugal, Bulgaria and India/British Empire, with around 900 copies in circulation.[13]

Clergymen such as the Presbyterian minister John Beveridge and the Anglican priest John Cyprian Rust (1841–1927) gave sermons during Esperanto congresses, as well as translated devotionals. The wider purposes of the use of Esperanto in the religious realm were perhaps best summarised in *Dia Regno*: to propagate Esperanto among churches, clergymen and missions, encourage the use of the language in churches and publish and disseminate religious texts through Esperanto.[14] In other words, promoting the language via faith was a key objective in addition to building religious vocabulary and showcasing Esperanto's literary value.

Prayers and excerpts from the Bible had already been translated into other constructed languages[15] such as Volapük[16] – which is not surprising, given that its initiator, Johann Martin Schleyer (1831–1912), was a Catholic priest who designed Volapük following a divine revelation.[17] Against this background, what would make Esperanto stand out would be the publication of the complete translation of both the Old and New Testaments.

It was John Cyprian Rust who took charge of formalising such an initiative. At the 1907 Universal Congress of Esperanto, Rust founded the Esperanto Bible Translation Committee. However, this first committee quickly dissolved, with some members resigning and others remaining inactive. We may not know whether Rust was of a particularly stubborn nature or on a mission, but we do know that he soon revived this initiative. In 1909, at the British Congress of Esperanto in Leeds, he recruited new members.[18] Since this new attempt took place during the British Congress, all members on this committee were British, but this time Rust's effort was successful and the translation work got under way.

This brings us back to the letter that opened this chapter. On 9 June 1909, William Main Page informed John Beveridge that the British Congress in

Leeds had elected the latter as a member of the *Biblia Komitato*, the Bible Translation Committee:

> Mi entreprenis ke membroj de la Edimburga grupo tradukos la Apokalipson, kaj post kiam la traduko estos farita mi sendos ĝin al vi por ekzamenado. Aliaj el la ĉeestantoj entreprenis traduki diversajn partojn de la Nova Testamento, kaj mi kredas ke laboro estos kompleta antaŭ la jarfino.[19]

Following the British Congress in Leeds, the communication between the Committee's voluntary translators was carried out via correspondence. John Cyprian Rust, convener of the Committee,[20] was an Anglican priest born in Colchester, Essex, who spent most of his life as the vicar of the Anglican church in Soham, Cambridgeshire. Rust shared the role of main proofreader and copyeditor of the translation[21] with Alfred Edward Wackrill (1862–1924), an engineer born in Leamington, Warwickshire, who had worked for years as land surveyor-general in Ceylon[22] before settling down in London in 1904.[23] John Beveridge, in turn, had been formally welcomed to the Committee by William Main Page, an English solicitor born in London who later moved to Edinburgh, building a career in the Scottish High Court.[24]

These lay translators actively engaged with Esperanto in different domains. Rust was responsible for the first known Christian preaching in Esperanto, on the occasion of the 1906 Universal Congress of Esperanto, in Geneva. Rust also wrote the first Order of Mass leaflet in Esperanto, which included a Christian hymn tune that he composed for an original Esperanto text.[25] This leaflet outlined the Christian Mass he celebrated during the 1907 Universal Congress of Esperanto, in Cambridge. Rust was also a regular contributor to *La Revuo*.

Contrasting with Rust's and Beveridge's religious and organisational contributions to Esperanto, Wackrill belonged to the first generation of members of the London Esperanto Club, founded in 1903, and became a member of the Akademio de Esperanto – the Academy of the Esperanto Language – in 1908.[26] Wackrill also held the editorship of the periodical *The British Esperantist*, translated English literary works such as Shakespeare's *Venecia Komercisto* (The Merchant of Venice) and compiled a list of root words that later became part of an official compendium to Zamenhof's *Universala Vortaro* (Universal Dictionary). Page, in turn, held significant roles such as editor of the periodicals *The Esperanto Monthly* and *The British Esperantist*. He was also co-editor of the *Enciklopedio de Esperanto* (1933), and acted as secretary of the Edinburgh Esperanto Society and president of the Scottish Esperanto Federation. Later, in 1926, Page was elected president of the Universal Congress of Esperanto held in Edinburgh. Even though not all these translators were active in religious spaces, they were heavily invested in various roles and offices in and around Esperanto.

The Committee's work initially focused on the New Testament. John Rust and William Page took the lead and approached potential contributors, divided the tasks to be carried out, and gathered and revised the translation drafts in consultation with other competent Esperanto speakers. In this regard, the letter that opened this chapter – in Esperanto, sent by Page to Beveridge on 9 June 1909 – indicated that John Beveridge was expected to also contribute to the revision of translation drafts. On the same day, Rust also wrote to Beveridge, in a letter in English, to assign him the translation of the First Epistle to Timothy (1 Timothy), the Second Epistle to Timothy (2 Timothy), and the Epistle to Titus. Interestingly, the labour of translating the New Testament – which would be conducted largely via the exchange of letters – formally began with the translation of the pastoral epistles, which take the shape of letters – from Paul the Apostle to Timothy and Titus.

In June 1909, despite recognising the arduous work ahead, both Rust and Page were optimistic that the New Testament would be fully translated by the end of that year.[27] Yet this proved to be too optimistic, and their expectation would not be met. The scriptures required their translators not only to be proficient writers of Esperanto but also proficient readers of Ancient Greek, as the Committee's work involved comparing the New Testament in Ancient Greek with its existing translations in Latin, English and, depending on each translator's skills, other modern languages.[28] As a clergyman passionate about languages and the words of the Lord, Beveridge was among the few who actually had the expertise required.

And the Word was progressively made flesh

In 1909, William Page and John Rust were in haste to translate the New Testament. Both sought to make the most of the momentum that Esperanto enjoyed in those years, and were hopeful that this translation would give more visibility to Esperanto among Christians and visibility to Christianity among Esperanto speakers. The Committee aimed to have the New Testament in Esperanto ready to be presented at major Esperanto and

Christian events in 1910, such as the British Congress of Esperanto, the Universal Congress of Esperanto and the World Missionary Conference. Page also planned to distribute copies of the translation to members of the Christian Commonwealth, along with an Esperanto key.[29]

The aim to have the translation of the Bible ready for the 1910 World Missionary Conference in Edinburgh sets this project into a wider context of religious dissemination and the mission movement. In this regard, the World Missionary Conference was an opportunity not to be missed. A previous missionary conference held in London in 1888 had brought together over 1,500 delegates from around 130 Protestant denominations, aiming to debate ways to spread both the gospel and civilisation as part of a global mission project. A second World Missionary Conference took place in New York in 1900. Over ten days in April and May 1900, more than 200,000 people attended the sessions held at Carnegie Hall – including prominent political figures such as Theodore Roosevelt, then Governor of New York.[30]

The World Missionary Conference in Edinburgh had been in the making for three years, and its planning must have been known to the group of Esperanto translators – not least as the conference's organising committee had met repeatedly in Edinburgh in the months leading up to 1910.[31] Starting in 1907, various committees worked on publications around major themes, all published as standalone volumes, such as *Carrying the Gospel to All the Non-Christian World*[32] and *The Church in the Mission Field*.[33] Having the Esperanto Bible translation, or at least the New Testament, ready by June 1910 would have meant an unprecedented opportunity to present Esperanto to the over 1,200 people participating in that conference.[34]

But when Randall Davidson – then Archbishop of Canterbury – opened the Edinburgh conference, the New Testament in Esperanto was not yet ready. The group of translators had encountered numerous setbacks. On several occasions, Rust apologised to Beveridge for delays in revising the translations – delays largely due to the fact that some of the submitted drafts were of such poor quality that Rust felt compelled to redo them entirely.[35]

Members of the Bible Translation Committee do not appear to have been selected primarily on the basis of their Esperanto proficiency.[36] The substandard quality of several translation drafts, as well as the frequent language mistakes in letters that Rust, Page and Beveridge received from other volunteers, attest to how the translation of the New Testament was carried out by Esperanto enthusiasts who were, ultimately, amateur linguists.

Yet this form of amateur approach in the religious milieu was not atypical. From the late nineteenth to the early twentieth century, numerous denominations were deeply invested in the globalisation of religion. While some of these denominations were more institutionalised and closely regulated – such as those behind the organisation of the World Missionary Conferences – others were less centralised and more focused on autonomous initiatives. These latter denominations provided groups of laypeople with room and encouragement to demonstrate their commitment to faith by taking their own initiative and spreading faith in a hands-on manner.[37] The Esperanto speakers in the Bible Translation Committee aligned primarily with the latter trend.

In the first decade of the twentieth century, despite setbacks and delays, Esperanto gradually established a presence in the Christian milieu. In addition to the previously mentioned periodicals *Espero Katolika* and *Dia Regno*, Christian Esperanto speakers came to organise regular meetings and worship services. They also held the First Congress of Catholic Esperantists in Paris, in 1910, where the Internacia Katolika Unuiĝo Esperantista (International Union of Catholic Esperantists, IKUE) was founded.[38] Realising that the New Testament would not be ready in time for the congresses in 1910, the Committee sought to translate at least the Sermon on the Mount.

The Sermon on the Mount, as well as the Gospel According to Matthew – the first book of the New Testament – had initially been assigned to an Episcopal clergyman from Edinburgh, who never sent his translations. These tasks were then transferred to John Beveridge.[39] Such incidents – from poor quality translations to contributions never received – reveal how the Bible Translation Committee was a loosely established network, rather than a fixed group. Several members joined the Committee but never effectively collaborated, while a number of Esperanto speakers and clergymen not formally on the Committee occasionally contributed through revising texts, forwarding correspondence or contacting publishers potentially interested in undertaking this project.

Meanwhile, Beveridge's translation of the Sermon on the Mount from the Ancient Greek original put him on the international map of Esperantujo.[40] Following the publication of the booklet, Beveridge received numerous compliments for his services to God and to Esperanto, as well as for 'perfectly preserving the sense of the Holy Scriptures'.[41] This praise came in postcards sent from places such as England, Belgium, Finland, the Russian Empire and Brazil.[42] Elsewhere, Esperanto periodicals advertised the leaflet, attesting to the wide reach of his translation.[43]

However, in February 1910, a new layer was added to the work of translating the New Testament. On 5 February, Rust received a letter from Ludwik Zamenhof in Esperanto, in which the latter asked whether someone had already been translating the Old Testament. If not, Zamenhof would be happy to do it himself.[44] Zamenhof's proposal caused a stir in the Committee, expressed in fast-paced correspondence exchanges among Rust, Beveridge, Wackrill and Page. The four translators were happy to accept Zamenhof's offer – as stated by Wackrill, in English, on 10 February: 'The main thing is: not to miss the opportunity of getting the work done by the most competent hand that the world is ever likely to produce. Time flies, and Zamenhof will not live forever. Every day lost now may mean a page of his great work is lost forever'. However, the same letter introduced Wackrill's caveats: 'Beg him to begin at once; but by all means submit a memorial, for his consideration, on the words *Elohim* and *Jehovah*', as well as 'To ask permission to criticise his manuscript is out of the question. He would take it as a veto on the whole work'.[45]

Despite the openness and humbleness that Zamenhof expressed in his letter offering to collaborate, there were limits to how much the Committee would be able to intervene in the translation made by Zamenhof – after all, he was the initiator of the language. More importantly, as summarised by Wackrill's first caveat, the Committee was particularly concerned about the extent to which Zamenhof's Old Testament would preserve or challenge certain Christian principles, which could end up making his translation incompatible with the New Testament. Ultimately, the question was: in case of disagreements, whose word would prevail, the words of the Lord or the words of the master – Esperanto's *majstro*?

The road to modernity, between the Lord and the master

The multilingualism of this endeavour was conspicuous. Having already translated eight books of the Old Testament – each published as a separate volume – Zamenhof continued translating the Old Testament from Hebrew, carefully comparing his translation with versions in several national languages.[46] This constant cross-referencing between languages left, in Zamenhof's version, traces of the Russian, Polish, German and French translations of the Old Testament, which confirms his use of multiple sources.[47] In the meantime, Beveridge translated and revised others' translations against the language versions he was able to read: Ancient Greek, Latin and English. Given Beveridge's fluency in and passion for Norwegian, he may also have used Bible translations in Norwegian.

In both the Old and New Testaments, these amateur Esperanto translators were keen on translating primarily from the original Hebrew and Ancient Greek texts. Refraining from using European national languages as bridge languages for these translations aimed to reinforce the image of Esperanto as an effective bridge language. The translators were eager to demonstrate that Esperanto could convey nuances of the Holy Scriptures just as effectively as any vernacular language. This emphasis on the original texts brings to the surface intriguing parallels between the Esperanto translation and concurrent approaches to modern Bible translation.

It is worth considering the controversies surrounding what constitutes 'the original text' of the New Testament. In the early Christian church, when apostolic letters were sent to congregations or individuals, copies would be made to facilitate the spread of their message. Over time, the work of scribes who copied these texts by hand would inevitably result in both accidental errors – like misspellings, additions and omissions – and intentional changes, some of which would occasionally be reproduced in subsequent copies produced from these versions.[48] After the invention of the printing press, when printed editions became the norm, several Greek manuscripts of the New Testament already existed, such as the Byzantine, Caesarean and Western texts. Despite the intentions of many translators and commentators to remain faithful to the original, it is difficult to pinpoint precisely what the term 'original' refers to, given that multiple 'originals' had emerged by the time of the Latin Vulgate and the Ancient Greek *Textus Receptus*.[49]

In a general sense, it can be argued that scholars and expert theologians devoted to translating the New Testament are concerned primarily with remaining faithful to the original language of the manuscript(s) available to them, aiming to preserve and explore the metaphors and figures of speech contained in the text.[50] By contrast, religious translators and missionaries tend to focus more on conveying the message itself, prioritising clarity and intelligibility for the purpose of spreading the word of God and facilitating conversion to Christianity.[51]

The links between faith and language were not new in John Beveridge's time. Focusing on the two main religions discussed in this chapter, Judaism became closely tied to the revival of Modern Hebrew as a spoken language, with Modern Hebrew consolidating its role as a unifying element within Jewish communities from the late nineteenth century onward.[52] Christianity, on the other hand, long associated with Latin, increasingly turned to the systematisation and documentation of indigenous languages as means for spreading the Christian faith throughout the twentieth century.[53] Almost paradoxically, Christianity's global reach drew on vernacular languages of local reach. Between 1900 and 1910 alone, 100 new translations of the Bible or parts thereof were published, followed by another 102 translations in the following decade. In contrast to the Esperanto translation project, these Bible translations were largely undertaken by linguistically well-trained missionaries – many of whom were theologians – with the help of expert language users and native speakers.[54]

The Esperanto translation of the Bible must be understood within this broader framework that connected faith and language with efforts to shape a particular European-inflected perception of what the 'global' is – or should be.[55] The Esperanto Bible is situated somewhere between the scholarly and the missionary paradigms of translation: on the one hand, several members of the Bible Translation Committee sought to spread the word of the Lord, focusing on preserving the message. On the other hand, an overarching goal of the Committee was to, by placing an emphasis on complex metaphors and figures of speech, spread the language of the master – *la majstro*, as Esperanto speakers occasionally referred to Zamenhof.[56]

Overall, however, the translation project was part and parcel of a much wider form of religious internationalism. In a period that saw the hardening of national borders, Esperanto and its transnational potential were envisioned as means to counter the growing patriotism of the time and foster the globalisation of a faith-based form of brotherhood or fellowship.[57]

In its first step, the Committee had to develop biblical terminology in Esperanto, in an exercise of language co-creation. As the person responsible for collecting all translation drafts, John Rust was particularly concerned with the Committee's reluctance to coin new vocabulary, as he expressed in a letter to John Beveridge, in English, on 5 October 1909:

> They [the Committee members] do not like *graco*, as it is not found in any authorized dictionary – Boirac has not admitted it into his new

> dictionary, which, I suppose, will be a standard. At the same time, I find that those who are actually engaged in the work of translating the N.T. [New Testament] are all anxious to have the special word *graco*, as no one word, nor even several words, can be found to correspond to the several uses of χαρις (e.g. see Coloss. iii.16-iv.6, Heb.x.29 – for difficult uses of χαρις to find an equivalent to).[58]

Rust continues, arguing that the Committee should accept *graco* because, even though dictionaries did not recognise it, this word had already been used in articles in magazines such as *Espero Katolika*.

Esperanto dictionaries were one of the key sources of vocabulary the Committee resorted to when deciding whether they needed to coin new terminology. Supportive of further vocabulary development, Rust was adamant that terms in Esperanto such as *kredi* and *fido* were acceptable, given how he deemed 'to believe' and 'faith' as appropriate English equivalents to both the Esperanto *kredi* and *fido* and the Greek πιστεύω and πίστη, respectively.

Zamenhof's words were a point in question. Occasionally, the Committee agreed with Zamenhof's terms, as Rust asserted: '*To stumble* is *falpuŝiĝi*. Dr. Z. has settled this for us – Prov.iv.19'.[59] At other times, Zamenhof's suggested translations stirred disagreements. The most significant one revolved around the term for 'God', as Rust discussed with Beveridge (in English) at length: 'Perhaps we may persuade him to drop his habit of translating יהוה by *Dio* which confuses the whole idea of God in the O.T. [Old Testament]'.[60]

This was also a concern for Wackrill – who, in an exchange in English with Rust, portrayed translation issues as divergences between the Jewish and Christian faiths:

> . . . it also appears that the Hebrew language often admits two or more interpretations of the same passage or word, sometimes carrying a considerable diversity of sense. [. . .] And it seems that there exists some anxiety lest Zamenhof should, in such passages, overlook the legitimate claims of Christianity to a rendering which would support the view that the Old Testament is a prophetic foreshadowing of the Christian dispensation.[61]

Along these lines, Zamenhof's translation of 'God' was also a bone of contention for Wackrill: '. . . by all means submit a memorial, for his consideration, on the words *Elohim* and *Jehovah*'. The translation and faith-related issues that emerged between Zamenhof and the Committee, then, were: first, who has the prerogative of being named *Dio* in the Esperanto Bible: Elohim, Jehovah (both from the Hebrew Bible/Old Testament) or God (the Christian God in the New Testament)?[62] Second, if the latter, who would challenge the *majstro*?

Given the archives available, the answer to the second question above may remain elusive. However, the first question can be partly answered by the outcome of the translation process. Ultimately, Jehovah was translated into Esperanto as *Eternulo* (the Eternal One). By contrast, Elohim and God were both rendered as *Dio* – which is consistent with the King James Bible's use of 'God'. Zamenhof also expressed his outright disapproval of the use of *Sinjoro* (Lord) as a trivial and profane way of referring to divine figures.[63]

Keeping the consistency and interfaith character of the Old and New Testaments was challenging. However, the pace of discussions over letter exchange and these translators' haste to publish the Esperanto Bible cut these debates short and sealed some disagreements over Jewish and Christian readings of the scriptures. Even so, sincerity in the use of words is a crucial aspect of the Christian faith. Accordingly, if sincerity points to the purity of the relationship between one's thoughts and words, likewise the translators of the Esperanto Bible faced the challenge of remaining faithful to both the Lord and the *majstro*.[64]

Ultimately, translating the Old and New Testaments into Esperanto was a paramount endeavour for situating Esperanto in wider imaginaries of modernity. At a time when Catholic missionaries translated the Bible into languages such as Guhu-Samane and brought Christianity to Papua New Guinea,[65] Dutch Protestants brought Calvinism to places such as the colonial Dutch East Indies.[66] By overriding local values and religious practices with Christianity, missionaries – largely in line with colonialist practices – perceived their work as paving the way to expanding modernity. Alongside the dissemination of technologies, European languages and Western 'civilising' values, this form of modernity was not at odds with faith. Rather, a more globalised and integrated world could also make room for religion.

This finds echoes in Esperanto and its Bible. Just as religious proselytising sought to turn non-Christians into part of global Christendom, Esperanto was perceived as a tool to bring into a global community those who were once relatively isolated in 'corners' of the world. In other words, the truth-claims associated with Christianity are meant to be as universal and globalising as the global reach and relevance that Esperanto speakers attached to this language. Hence, going beyond poor translations that had to be redone and disagreements over vocabulary development, the very existence of an Esperanto Bible points to the venture of imagining a global community through a world religion and an international language. With the translation of the Bible and of several secular books, this version of modernity sought to make room for atheism as much as for any religious faith.[67]

A Presbyterian, an Anglican and a Jew walk into a Translation Committee

After three years in the making, the work of the Bible Translation Committee culminated in the publication of the translated New Testament as *La Nova Testamento de nia Sinjoro kaj Savanto Jesuo Kristo* in 1912.[68] With the translation of the New Testament becoming available much earlier than the Old Testament, the Committee resorted to several biblical societies to support its publication. Negotiations led by William Page secured the support of the British and Foreign Bible Society, which undertook this publication, whose final revision was carried out by John Rust and Alfred Wackrill.[69]

The Old Testament faced more setbacks to come into being.[70] On 3 March 1915, Zamenhof sent a letter to Rust – in French this time – eagerly announcing that he had finished his translation:

> Cher Monsieur! – J'ai le grand plaisir de pouvoir vous annoncer que l'Ancien Testament est déjà en entier traduit (et écrit à la machine). [. . .] Malheureusement je ne peux pas vous envoyer la traduction à présent, car notre poste n'expédie rien (pendant la guerre) qui est écrit en Esperanto. Par conséquent je suis obligé d'attendre jusqu'à la fin de la guerre.[71]

As discussed in Chapter 1, postcards were key for the early materialisations of the Esperanto language community. However, the First World War limited how far words could go via postal services.[72] Even though the Old Testament had been fully translated, Zamenhof was unable to send the manuscript from the Russian Empire to Britain.[73] Writing to Rust in French – which, unlike Esperanto, was permitted by the Russian postal service – Zamenhof conveyed good and bad news about a translation that would only reach the Bible Translation Committee in 1919 – after the war had ended, and two years after Zamenhof's death.

Between 1919 and 1925, a partly renewed Bible Translation Committee revised Zamenhof's translation. They put together both the eight books of the Old Testament that had been previously translated by Zamenhof and published with Hachette, and the remaining books received in 1919.[74] This project of harmonising the language used in the Old and New Testaments[75] came to fruition in 1926, when both Testaments were at last published together under the title *La Sankta Biblio: Malnova kaj Nova Testamentoj tradukitaj el la originalaj lingvoj* (The Holy Bible: The Old and New Testaments Translated from the Original Languages).[76]

Key actors behind the endeavour, including John Cyprian Rust and John Beveridge, were still part of the Committee then. They worked alongside old and new Committee members such as William Main Page, H. O. Allbrook, M. J. Elliott, C. Gaydou, T. S. Lindsay, J. E. McFadyen, A. Poynder, E. J. Price and W. Bailey. Of the members, the Scotland-based ones were Beveridge, Page and McFadyen.[77] Most of these translators were Protestant clergymen from different denominations and all of them were based in Britain. This was one of the reasons why this first translation of the Holy Bible became known as *La Londona Biblio* (The London Bible).

Interestingly, even though the Bible Translation Committee was entirely made of men, the funds that covered the publication expenses of the 1926 Bible came from two Quaker women: Hannah Priscilla Peckover (1833–1931) and Algerina Peckover (1841–1927).[78] The sisters followed the translation project from its first steps. Hailing from a wealthy banking family, they not only had the means to financially support the project but also had their own personal interests in seeing the project succeed. Hannah Priscilla Peckover, who learned Esperanto late in life, had a longstanding affiliation with the peace movement and was one of the figureheads behind the Women's Local Peace Association from the late 1870s. Her own engagement as a Quaker and peace activist certainly resonated with the idea of an international auxiliary language that could allow the spread of the message of peace in the Gospel.[79]

The dedication of the Esperanto Bible took place at the Protestant St Giles' Cathedral. Located on the Royal Mile in the heart of Edinburgh, this cathedral was also at the heart of the sixteenth-century Scottish Reformation, serving as John Knox's parish church.[80] The event took place on 1 August 1926, featuring John Beveridge as one of the four ministers conducting the ceremonial service. This dedication was a prominent event at the Eighteenth Universal Congress of Esperanto held in Edinburgh that summer.

The 1926 *London Bible* marked the first complete Esperanto translation of the Holy Bible. However, it was not a single, unified translation; rather, it was an assemblage of texts translated from various 'originals' and influenced by prior translations into several European languages. Nor was the *London Bible* the only Holy Bible in Esperanto. Individual Esperanto speakers – particularly those affiliated with the International Union of Catholic Esperantists and the International League of Christian Esperantists – continued to produce essays on religious themes and proposed revised translations of books from both the Old and New Testaments. The most recent complete translation of the Bible into Esperanto was published in 2006 by Gerrit Berveling,[81] a Remonstrant minister and theologian, who drew on the Latin Vulgate and the *London Bible* to produce his revised translation.[82]

Translating the scriptures was a means of conveying a certain message both to Esperanto speakers and to the world about how inclusive this constructed language could be. While crafting this message through correspondence exchange, vocabulary development and translation, the individuals behind this project were also developing Esperanto-speaking interfaith networks.

As discussed earlier, translations of the Bible into national and vernacular languages were meant to make the scriptures compelling and intelligible to individuals from specific world regions – as is the case of the missionary work to spread Christianity among indigenous peoples.[83] Meanwhile, writing in – or translating into – Esperanto meant addressing a transnational readership, composed of readers from different national and ethnic backgrounds and speakers of different first languages.[84] An attention to such a diverse readership also meant being mindful of diverse faiths. Ultimately, this translation effort brought together Jews, Catholics and Protestants of several denominations – Episcopalians, Presbyterians, Anglicans and Remonstrants – all the while being funded by Quakers. Such a work, then, involved bridging several religions and denominations, deities that could potentially be called *Dio*, languages and challenging setbacks concerning cross-border postal services.

Concluding remarks

Postcards may be ephemera, just as perhaps these networks may not have lasted for longer than this immediate collaboration. Yet the book this collaboration produced emerges as a long-standing result of this community-building practice. While Esperanto speakers seemed to 'simply' exchange letters, they developed the language, produced knowledge and gave flesh and bones to this language community.

While regular, face-to-face expressions of Esperanto's internationality were limited to the week-long Universal Congresses of Esperanto, held once a year, communication technologies such as postcards served as a primary means for this community to endure in the long term. Interestingly, all the translation work was carried out via correspondence, and there is no evidence that these translators ever met in person.

In developing vocabulary, these translators also developed Esperanto-speaking interfaith networks, bringing together several religious denominations, languages and religious texts. Even though the process analysed here primarily concerns the Esperanto translations of the Old and New Testaments taking place in the early twentieth century, the revision of scriptures and celebration of Masses in Esperanto continues to date.

Producing this community also involved establishing the connections and reading materials that would, ultimately, give substance to a form of Esperanto-mediated modernity. Such a form of modernity did not have to be secular but would necessarily be global and inclusive, making room for potentially anyone. 'Anyone' here is understood as a person that could be anywhere, from any background, and who could learn the language, join the language community, and even – who knows – become Christian. Like Christianity – or science, for that matter – Esperanto was powered by a set of internationalist values that claimed this language's potential relevance to all human beings – ideas of modernity that were integral to the discourses and imaginaries of early twentieth-century Esperanto speakers.

Notes

1 Émile Boirac, *Plena Vortaro Esperanto-Esperanta kaj Esperanto-Franca. Unua Parto* (Dijon: Darantière, 1909); Émile Boirac, *Plena Vortaro Esperanto-Esperanta kaj Esperanto-Franca. Dua Parto* (Dijon: Darantière, 1910).

2 William Allen Smalley, *Translation as Mission: Bible Translation in the Modern Missionary Movement* (Macon, GA: Mercer University Press, 1991), 33.

3 The booklet in Russian was subsequently translated into French, German, Polish (in 1887) and English (in 1888) – before being revised and published in a multilingual edition in 1905. See Zamenhof, *Fundamento*.

4 See, for instance, Ludwik Lejzer Zamenhof, *Fundamenta Krestomatio de la Lingvo Esperanto* (Paris: Hachette, 1905).

5 Ludwik Lejzer Zamenhof, *Dr. Esperanto's International Language: Introduction and Complete Grammar*, trans. R. H. Geoghegan (Warsaw: self-publication, 1887), page succeeding the title page.

6 In English: 'No book is as well known throughout the civilised world as the Bible, and if we could show the world that Esperanto has the translation of the entire Bible, this would be a very powerful propaganda tool for us. [. . .] For most of the current cultural languages, the Bible has been the main foundation on which languages have taken the shape of literature and developed; therefore, it will undoubtedly be very important for our language to possess that foundation, with its many words and expressions that have become an elemental necessity for every contemporary cultural language.' Ludwik Lejzer Zamenhof, 'Antaŭparolo al la Genezo', *La Revuo*, IV, 1909–10, 337–8.

7 The Jewish Hebrew Bible corresponds roughly to the Protestant Old Testament, with variations based on religious denomination. The Hebrew Bible and the Protestant Old Testament have the same books (chapters), but these are divided differently, such that the former consists of thirty-nine books and the latter has twenty-four. By contrast, the Catholic Bible consists of forty-six books, including the seven Deuterocanonical books that Protestants and Jews regard as apocrypha. The New Testament, on the other hand, is canonical only to the Christian faith and comprises twenty-seven books.

8 The books of the Bible published by Hachette between 1907 and 1914 as separate volumes were: *Predikanto* (Ecclesiastes), *Psalmaro* (Psalms), *Genezo* (Genesis), *Eliro* (Exodus), *Levido* (Leviticus), *Nombroj* (Numbers), *Readmono* (Deuteronomy) and *La sentencoj de Salomono* (Proverbs).

9 In English: 'May those who are religious forgive me that I – being neither a pastor nor a specialist in religious matters – undertook the task of translating a religious work. However, I can absolve myself by explaining that I translated the Psalms not as a religious work but as an important work of humankind's literature. For purely religious purposes, another translation may appear sooner or later, crafted by clerical specialists.' Ludwik Lejzer Zamenhof, *La Psalmaro el la Biblio. El la originalo tradukis d-ro L. L. Zamenhof* (Paris: Hachette, 1908), 1.

10 E. Neumark, translator, *La Libro Ruth* (Nuremberg: Presejo de W. Tümmel, 1893).

11 It is worth noting how controversial the term 'original' can be regarding the Bible, as we will discuss shortly.

12 W. B. Mielck and F. Stephan, trans, *La evangelio Sankta Mateo laŭ Dro Martin Luther* (Leipzig: J.C. Hinrich'sche Buchhandlung, 1906).

13 *Dia Regno*, February 1910, 13.

14 *Dia Regno*, January 1911, 5.

15 It is worth noting the popularity, among creators and speakers of constructed languages, of the Genesis excerpt about the Tower of Babel.

16 The First Epistle of John was translated into Volapük by Johann Martin Schleyer. See Johann Martin Schleyer, *Pened balid Yoliánesà* (Konstanz: VOL, 1888).

17 Garvía, *Esperanto and Its Rivals*, 39.

18 John Beveridge Collection, Ms36242/151.

19 In English: 'I undertook that members of the Edinburgh group will translate the Apocalypse, and after the translation is done, I will send it to you for review. Other attendees committed to translate various parts of the New Testament, and I believe the work will be complete before the end of the year.' John Beveridge Collection, Ms36242/151.

20 John Beveridge Collection, Ms36244/19; Ms36244/16.

21 John Beveridge Collection, Ms36242/163.

22 Royal Society for the Encouragement of Arts, Manufactures and Commerce. 'List of the Council and Officers for the 145th Session, 1898–9', *The Journal of the Society of Arts* 47, no. 2400 (1898), 1–44.

23 Alfred E. Wackrill, *Kelkaj impresoj de Hindujo. Literatura almanako* (Paris: Presa Esperantista Societo, 1909), 67.

24 See Kökény and Bleier, *Enciklopedio*.

25 The leaflet was translated, edited and partly authored by John Cyprian Rust, *Ordo de Diservo, Laŭ la Preĝlibro de la Angla Eklezio* (London: La Tria Kongreso, 1907).

26 Beveridge's religious and organisational contributions to Esperanto were covered in detail in previous chapters.

27 John Beveridge Collection, Ms36242/150 and Ms36242/151, respectively.

28 Regarding English, the King James Bible was their key point of comparison.

29 John Beveridge Collection, Ms36242/162.

30 On the Edinburgh 1910 conference see Brian Stanley, *The World Missionary Conference, Edinburgh 1910* (Grand Rapids, MI: William B. Eerdmans, 2009); Thomas A. Askew, 'The New York 1900 Ecumenical Missionary Conference: A Centennial Reflection'. *International Bulletin of Missionary Research* 24, no. 4 (2000): 146–54.

31 Brian Stanley, 'Scotland and the World Missionary Conference, Edinburgh 1910', *Records of the Scottish Church History Society* 41 (2012): 113–32, here 118–19.

32 *Report of Commission I: Carrying the Gospel to all the non-Christian World; with Supplement: Presentation and Discussion of the Report in the Conference on 15th June 1910* (Edinburgh: Publ. for the World Missionary Conference by Oliphant, Anderson & Ferrier, 1910).

33 *Report of Commission II: The Church in the Mission Field* (Edinburgh: Publ. for the World Missionary Conference by Oliphant, Anderson & Ferrier, 1910).

34 Stanley, *The World Missionary Conference*, 1–12.

35 See John Beveridge Collection, Ms36242/156.

36 See Forster, *The Esperanto Movement*, 368. Forster advances a similar argument regarding Zamenhof: neither Zamenhof nor the early members of Esperanto's Language Committee were professional linguists. Regardless of their good intentions and devotion to the language, they were at most amateur linguists and Esperanto enthusiasts.

37 Abigail Green and Vincent Viaene, eds. *Religious Internationals in the Modern World: Globalization and Faith Communities since 1750* (Houndmills: Palgrave Macmillan, 2012), 1–2, 14–15.

38 Ulrich Matthias, *Esperanto: La nova latino de la Eklezio* (Antwerp: Flandra Esperanto-Ligo, 2002).

39 John Beveridge Collection, Ms36242/163-164.

40 John Beveridge, *La Prediko sur la Monto. Tradukis el la originala greka teksto Pastro John Beveridge* (London: British Esperanto Association / Edinburgh: Andrew Elliot, 1910).

41 John Beveridge Collection, Ms36242/170.

42 John Beveridge Collection, Ms36242/170, Ms36242/181, Ms36242/172, Ms36242/199, Ms36242/245, Ms36242/169 (four from the Russian Empire, one from Tbilisi, and one from Warsaw, the latter sent by Zamenhof), and Ms36242/175 (from Superaguy, Brazil).

43 See, for instance, *Dia Regno*, June 1910, 47; *Amerika Esperantisto*, December 1911, 30.

44 John Beveridge Collection, Ms36242/157.

45 John Beveridge Collection, Ms36242/159.

46 Ludwik Lejzer Zamenhof, *La Psalmaro el la Biblio. El la originalo tradukis d-ro L. L. Zamenhof* (Paris: Hachette, 1908), 1.

47 Douglas Bartlett Gregor, *La Esperanta Traduko de la Malnova Testamento: Dek-biblia konkordanco de 518 diskutindaj versoj* (Scheveningen: Heroldo de Esperanto, 1958); 'Arieh ben Guni, Recenzo: La Esperanta traduko de la Malnova Testamento', *Nica literatura revuo* 5, no. 5 (1960), 194–7.

48 Bruce Metzger, *The Text of the New Testament: Its Transmission, Corruption, and Restoration* (Oxford: Oxford University Press, 1968).

49 Bruce Metzger, *A Textual Commentary on the Greek New Testament* (London and New York: United Bible Societies, 1971), xv–xxiv.

50 Bruce Metzger, *The Bible in Translation: Ancient and English Versions* (Grand Rapids, MI: Baker Academic, 2001).

51 William Allen Smalley, *Translation as Mission: Bible Translation in the Modern Missionary Movement* (Macon, GA: Mercer University Press, 1991).

52 Richard E. Wood, 'A Voluntary, Non-ethnic, Non-territorial Speech Community', in *Sociolinguistic Studies in Language Contact: Methods and Cases*, ed. William F. Mackey and Jacob Ornstein (The Hague: Mouton, 1979), 441–2; Liora Halperin, 'Other Tongues: The Place of Foreign Language in Hebrew Culture', in *Reflections on Knowledge and Language in Middle Eastern Societies*, ed. Bruno De Nicola, Yonatan Mendel and Husain Qutbuddin (Newcastle upon Tyne: Cambridge Scholars Publishing, 2010), 228–47.

53 See David Stoll, 'The Summer Institute of Linguistics and Indigenous Movements', *Latin American Perspectives* 9, no. 2 (1982), 84–99; Courtney Handman, *Critical Christianity: Translation and Denominational Conflict in Papua New Guinea* (Oakland: University of California Press, 2015); Noo Supu, *A Triglot Dictionary. Compiled by Dr. Ernest L. Richert and Ttopoqogo Hoopusus* (Ukarumpa: Summer Institute of Linguistics, 2002).

54 Smalley, *Translation as Mission*, 28–9; Frederick Aldridge, *The Development of the Wycliffe Bible Translators and the Summer Institute of Linguistics, 1934–1982* (PhD dissertation, University of Stirling, 2012).

55 Green and Viane, *Religious Internationals*, 1–2.

56 See, for instance, Julio Baghy's well-known poem titled 'La Majstro mortis', on the death of Zamenhof. Julio Baghy, *Preter la vivo* (Budapest: Literatura Mondo, 1922).

57 Green and Viane, *Religious Internationals*, 7–8.

58 John Beveridge Collection, Ms36242/155.

59 John Beveridge Collection, Ms36242/155.

60 John Beveridge Collection, Ms36242/157ii.

61 John Beveridge Collection, Ms36242/159.

62 Michael J. Stahl, *The 'God of Israel' in History and Tradition* (Leiden: Brill, 2021), 52–144.

63 Ludwik Lejzer Zamenhof, 'Antaŭparolo al la Genezo', *La Revuo*, IV, 1909–10, 337–8.

64 Webb Keane, *Christian Moderns: Freedom and Fetish in the Mission Encounter* (Berkeley: University of California Press, 2007).

65 Handman, *Critical Christianity.*

66 Keane, *Christian Moderns.*

67 Tomoko Masuzawa, *The Invention of World Religions or, How European Universalism Was Preserved in the Language of Pluralism* (Chicago: University of Chicago Press, 2005); Green and Viaene, *Religious Internationals.*

68 *La Nova Testamento de nia Sinjoro kaj Savanto Jesuo Kristo* (London: La Brita kaj Eksterlanda Biblia Societo / Edinburgh and Glasgow: Nacia Biblia Societo de Skotlando, 1912).

69 John Beveridge Collection, Ms36242/168.

70 The Old Testament that Zamenhof translated was the one commonly used by Jews and Protestants, containing thirty-nine books and leaving out the Deuterocanonical books, which both Jews and Protestants regard as apocrypha.

71 In English: 'Dear Sir, I am very pleased to inform you that the Old Testament has already been fully translated (and typed). [. . .] Unfortunately, I cannot send you the translation at present, as our postal service does not dispatch anything (during the war) written in Esperanto. Consequently, I am obliged to wait until the end of the war.' See also Public Letter from Ludwik Lejzer Zamenhof to John Cyprian Rust, *The British Esperantist* 11, no. 124 (1915), 66. Ludwig Lejzer Zamenhof, 'Al pastro J. Cyprian Rust, "Pri la Malnova Testamento"', in *Originala Verkaro*, 472.

72 On censorship of Esperanto, and censorship more generally during the war, see O'Keeffe, *Esperanto and Languages of Internationalism*, 53–8; John T. Smith, 'Russian Military Censorship during the First World War', *Revolutionary Russia* 14, no. 1 (2001): 71–95.

73 A certain M. Fred, who otherwise eludes the record, produced the first translation of some of the Old Testament books that Zamenhof used to ground his own translation. See Zamenhof, 'Al Pastro J. Cyprian Rust', in *Originala Verkaro*, 472.

74 Thomas Creusot, *L'utopie sous presse. Éditer l'espéranto en France (1897–1939)* (Master's dissertation, École nationale des chartes, 2022).

75 Gregor, *La Esperanta Traduko*, 43.

76 *La Sankta Biblio: Malnova kaj Nova Testamentoj tradukitaj el la originalaj lingvoj* (London: Brita kaj Alilanda Biblio Societo / Edinburgh and Glasgow: Nacia Biblia Societo de Skotlando, 1926).

77 John Beveridge Collection, Ms36244/19.

78 See Matthias, *Esperanto*; Garvía, *Esperanto and Its Rivals,* 110.

79 Heloise Brown, *The Truest Form of Patriotism: Pacifist Feminism in Britain, 1870–1902* (Manchester: Manchester University Press, 2003), 79–98.

80 Michael Lynch, 'John Knox, Minister of Edinburgh and Commissioner of the Kirk', in *John Knox and the British Reformations*, ed. Roger Mason (London: Routledge, 2018), 242–67.

81 Geoffrey Greatex, 'Translations of Virgil into Esperanto', in *Virgil and His Translators*, ed. Susanna Braund and Zara Martirosova Torlone (Oxford: Oxford University Press, 2018), 124–35.

82 Ludwik Lejzer Zamenhof, Gerrit Berveling, John Cyprian Rust, John Beveridge and C. G. Wilkinson, trans., *Biblio* (Dobřichovice: Kava-Pech, 2006).

83 See Handman, *Critical Christianity*; Keane, *Christian Moderns*.

84 Ian Richmond, 'Esperanto Literature and the International Reader', in *Aspects of Internationalism: Language and Culture*, ed. Ian Richmond (Lanham, MD: University Press of America, 1993), 103–18; Kevin Grieves, 'Esperanto Journalism and Readers as "Managers": A Transnational Participatory Audience'. *Media History* 27, no. 1 (2020): 1–13.

Conclusion: the history of international communication via postcards and Esperanto

John Beveridge could have joined a philatelic society instead of exchanging postal stamps with Esperanto speakers. Likewise, Lois Beveridge could have travelled abroad simply to visit Dresden, rather than to attend an Esperanto congress, and Heather Beveridge could have published journal articles in French. However, Esperanto, postcards and international congresses were the means chosen by the Beveridge family to transcend their provincial, ordinary lives in Dundee. In this way, Esperanto was one among several entry points these actors had at their disposal to engage with modernity, multilingualism and internationalism during the waves of globalisation at the turn of the twentieth century. Analysing these global phenomena through the standpoints and language choices of these actors is what provides us with an alternative vantage point to the history of international communication.

Grounded in the postcards, publications and archival traces left by John, Lois and Heather Beveridge, this book has revolved around how these actors used Esperanto to convey their messages and communicate their imaginaries. Following these individuals enabled us to address a number of questions. First, at a time when postal services, steamships and the telephone set the pace of modernity and globalisation, what role could language play amidst this increasingly international(ist) scenario? Second, given that international auxiliary languages like Esperanto were tailor-made for cross-border communication, how was Esperanto effectively used and what were its speakers doing with it? Third, why and how would people from relatively small places across Europe invest their time and energy in learning and using such a language? Fourth, what kinds of grassroots internationalism could 'global' languages afford ordinary people such as the Beveridges?

Chapter 1 brought us to small places to reveal the modus operandi of a language community in the making. Through the postcards exchanged between Esperanto speakers from rural areas and small towns in Scotland, Bulgaria, Finland and Austria–Hungary, we found how this language gained ground not despite the geographical dispersal of its speakers, but precisely because of it. Had Esperanto become an official or commonly spoken language somewhere, it would have lost its prominence as an international auxiliary language. As such, correspondence exchange became a means for people from small places to carve out a space for themselves in international communication. Through postcards, a clergyman living on Scotland's east coast got a glimpse of Sweden's architecture and the kinds of outfits people going on a boat excursion in rural Finland would wear. In satisfying their desires for worldliness, Esperanto pen pals used this language as a means to connect with fellow speakers who were curious about what architecture, clothing and poetry on the other side of the continent looked and read like without leaving their homes – all the while making friends and, unintentionally, contributing to making Esperantujo.

Chapter 2 foregrounded an ordinary Esperanto-speaking household in Dundee, following the ways in which three individuals made sense of speaking an international language locally. After all, to engage with grassroots internationalism, one needed to have the means to do so – including time, money, energy and language proficiency. Hence, before Esperanto became a fully fledged international auxiliary language, it ensured its existence at the local level through people buying language learning materials, studying as autodidacts and joining local clubs to practise the language and make friends. However, for language learning materials, clubs and congresses to exist, Esperanto speakers must make an effort to constantly create and recreate the spaces, publications and occasions on which the language could be used. To some, speaking and writing in Esperanto rapidly turned from a leisure activity into a time-consuming commitment that involved breathing life again and again into the language community.

Chapter 3 shifted our focus to key actors that have been systematically neglected in scholarship: Esperanto-speaking women. If they made up around half of the speakers of the language in the early twentieth century, why is the history of Esperanto so prominently focused on male actors – from Ludwik Zamenhof to the male founders of Esperanto clubs and male editors of magazines? The lives of Esperanto-speaking women in Scotland led us to the plays they performed, associations they headed, and the literary and scientific texts they produced. As women engaged with the language in multiple ways, they also enacted alternative lifestyles, using Esperanto to either find their place in society as teachers and club members or to challenge social conventions of the time when travelling abroad unaccompanied or standing out in male-dominated scientific circles.

In turn, Chapter 4 considered the wider power dynamics involving key Esperanto pioneers – such as Ludwik Zamenhof – and ordinary language speakers as they co-produced the translation of the Bible into Esperanto. Translation and interpreting emerged as major activities among Esperanto speakers, given how the creation of fully developed Esperanto-speaking spaces first required that all content be rendered into Esperanto.[1] While groups of voluntary translators worked to produce the Old and New Testaments in Esperanto, they also had to coin new terms to name things not initially named by Zamenhof, which fleshed out power imbalances in the process of navigating between various language skills and faiths. As a result, producing such a book entailed developing interfaith networks, new vocabulary and the very Esperantujo that was forged through translation.

Combined, these chapters allowed us to narrate an alternative history of international communication in three ways. First, while placing language at the centre of our approach to communication, we have deliberately not focused on the most hegemonic languages at the time, such as French and English. Choosing to concentrate on Esperanto instead led us to explore grassroots internationalism from the perspective of those who communicated across borders by trying to bypass the more explicit power relations conveyed through the use of national languages made global via colonialism and imperialism.

Second, the standpoint adopted in this book allowed for a grassroots history of Esperanto beyond the commonplace historiographical approach that takes Ludwik Zamenhof, other well-known Esperanto speakers, Universal Congresses and major Esperanto associations in Paris, Geneva or Prague as its centrepieces. Rather, we provided elements for a history of how this language gained ground among ordinary people, through centring on the small places and grassroots approaches to internationalism that constituted the core of what turned Esperanto into a fully developed international auxiliary language through correspondence exchange.

Third, our scale of analysis, centred on individuals and small places, enabled highlighting forms of language use that made Esperanto what it effectively is: a transnational and grassroots phenomenon. After all, once this constructed language is out, it takes a life of its own, becoming independent from Ludwik Zamenhof and the top-down ventures of major Esperanto associations. Without substantial backing from state agents or international bodies, Esperanto relied on people voluntarily opting in and willingly learning the language, oftentimes as autodidacts. People – men and women alike, however obvious such a reminder might read – were drawn to Esperanto for various reasons, and even if we may not always have sources that attest to their motivations to do so, we are still able to map what they achieved through their use of the language. In this regard, a curious conclusion that our actors' narratives point us to is: the process of becoming an Esperanto speaker appears to subvert a clear relationship of cause and consequence, as numerous Esperanto pioneers seemed to have come across the language, decided to learn it, and only at a later point figured out what to do with it and through it.

Having the freedom to choose a language and experiment with it could appear entertaining at first glance. Yet it involved a significant commitment. Unlike national and regional languages – which one knows in advance where they are spoken – Esperanto is spoken by a geographically dispersed community, with speakers potentially everywhere, but concentrated nowhere. Thus, speaking or writing in Esperanto also entailed being constantly involved in the hard work of producing and reproducing the clubs, publications and events that came to provide speakers with occasions to use the language. This maintenance work was not an easy feat, requiring people to perform the roles of president of clubs and associations, translator and author of published volumes, and organiser of congresses.

This book points to how small places should not be perceived as isolated, marginal or peripheral. Beginning our journey from Scotland's east coast, seemingly on the fringes of international communication and globalisation, we found that this relatively small place was not isolated at all. There was an intense circulation of people and commodities in Dundee's port that turned it into an international and multilingual space, even though a significant portion of the city's population was not directly involved in international trade. For those who were not dock workers, sailors and merchants, Esperanto was one way of expanding the intellectual and cultural boundaries of one's provincial lifestyle. Likewise, John Beveridge's correspondents in Harmanli or Kymi may have lived in small places but also used Esperanto and postcards to have experiences that made them anything but isolated. Along these lines, these people and places constituted nodes in a widespread network, which calls into question the dichotomy of centre versus peripheries/margins.

This emphasis on ordinary people substantiates a novel approach not only to the history of international communication and Esperanto but, more broadly, to a transnational history of Europe. Through grand narratives about emerging telegraph networks, increasingly popular trips via steamships and diesel trains, and standardisation efforts – aiming to standardise from units of measurement to scientific language and the pronunciation of words in everyday parlance – technological achievements in the late nineteenth and early twentieth centuries came to characterise this period in Western European history as *La Belle Époque*. However, as we showed in the introduction, the wonders of *La Belle Époque* did not reach everyone the same way across Europe. The women who worked in jute mills in Dundee did not necessarily experience the marvels showcased at Universal Exhibitions in Chicago or Paris. Similarly, our actors in Dundee, Harmanli or Kymi neither witnessed the pioneering aeroplane flights nor crossed continents more than once in their lifetimes. Against this backdrop, our narrative written not about but around the Beveridge family reveals how ordinary people were effectively experiencing the technologies, values and expectations that underpinned the wave of globalisation at the turn of the twentieth century.

Finally, one might be wondering – and rightly so – what happened to John Beveridge after he translated the New Testament, or to Lois Beveridge after she earned her Esperanto qualifications and spent years teaching the language in Dundee and Perth. In 1914, when the First World War broke out, John Beveridge was caught in Norway and struggled to travel back to Scotland. These circumstances increased his interest in the Norwegian language, traditions, religion and folklore and, in the following years, he would strengthen his contact with Norwegian clergymen and theologians. In 1938, the many visits of John Beveridge to Free Churches in Norway, the newspaper articles he wrote in Norwegian, the religious exchanges he established through correspondence and the Norwegian clergymen he welcomed in his Dundee home culminated in the Norwegian King Haakon VII awarding Beveridge the Order of St Olav, a high civilian honour.[2] Between 1914 and 1943 – the year when John Beveridge died of natural causes – we lose the paper trail of his engagement with Esperanto, which leaves it unclear whether he had reduced his use of the language or whether these further documents have not been preserved.

In the meantime, Lois Beveridge combined the skills she developed teaching Esperanto with her interest in religion and spent over thirty years doing missionary work in places ranging from China to the British Gold Coast, after which we also lose track of her internationalist endeavours. Heather Beveridge, in turn, largely eludes the record, which prevents us from knowing where – if somewhere – her 1908 journal article brought her. However, what happened to Esperanto after we lost track of the Beveridge family?

The narrative of this book covered only the beginning: the thriving early decades of this language. Just as the First World War delayed John Beveridge's trip back to Scotland in 1914, it also hindered the realisation of the Eleventh Universal Congress of Esperanto, due to take place in Edinburgh in 1915. But the war did not put an end to Esperanto. In effect, in the interwar period, manual labourers and anti-nationalist activists embraced Esperanto as a non-nationalist tool to oppose nationalist rivalries, leading to the emergence of left-leaning and worker's Esperanto associations and congresses.[3] Meanwhile, the highly anticipated yet previously cancelled Universal Congress of Esperanto in Edinburgh finally took place in 1926, with John Beveridge conducting an ecumenical service in Esperanto during the congress. Shortly after, with the Second World War breaking out, Esperanto speakers were persecuted by totalitarian regimes in Europe, Asia and the Americas for pursuing a kind of internationalism that was deemed 'dangerous' during wartime.[4]

In the second half of the twentieth century, in turn, Esperanto speakers came to increasingly associate the language with variations of 'neutrality': in 1954, UNESCO issued a motion recognising the similarities between the agendas of UNESCO and the World Esperanto Association.[5] Subsequently, in the Cold War period, periodicals for the youth attempted to portray Esperanto as a neutral alternative for international communication – an alternative language that could circumvent 'capitalist' English, backed by the US, and 'socialist' Russian, backed by the Soviet Union.[6]

In recent years, in turn, Esperanto speakers saw the rise of online language learning through mobile phone apps such as Duolingo, and the ongoing Universal Congresses of Esperanto – whose annual realisation was only interrupted during the First World War – reached the African continent for the first time in 2025, when the congress was held in Arusha, Tanzania.

Yet this is another story. The history of Esperanto continues, and the period this book covers has revealed just a snapshot of it. Blending even newer translations of the Bible, original literature from William Auld – a three-time Nobel Prize nominee for his works in Esperanto – and translations of J. R. R. Tolkien's *The Lord of Rings* – as well as with speakers using not only postcards but also social media platforms to communicate – the language is around and (well) alive, continuing to thrive through the use of emergent communication technologies and securing its place in supporting grassroots internationalism amidst ever-returning nationalist rivalries and xenophobia.

Notes

1 Manuela Burghelea, 'On Not Being Lost in Translation: Creative Strategies to Approach Multiculturalism in Esperanto', *Język, Komunikacja, Informacja* 13 (2018): 159–74.

2 John Beveridge Collection, Ms36244/15; *Norsk Tidend*, 1 July 1942, 5.

3 Anne-Sophie Markov, *Le Mouvement International des Travailleurs Espérantistes, 1918–1939* (Master's Dissertation, Université de Versailles Saint-Quentin-en-Yvelines, 1999).

4 Lins, *Dangerous Language: Hitler and Stalin*; Lins, *Dangerous Language: Decline of Stalinism*; Lins, *La Danĝera Lingvo*; Rapley, *Green Star Japan*; Fians, 'O que falar em esperanto quer dizer'.

5 Forster, *The Esperanto Movement*, 242–8.

6 Guilherme Fians, 'Neutralizing the Political: Language Ideology as Censorship in Esperanto Youth Media during the Cold War', *Journal of Linguistic Anthropology* 34, no. 2 (2024), 200–19.

Bibliography

Primary sources

Manuscripts from the John Beveridge Collection, University of St Andrews Special Collections

- Postcards: Ms36242/112, Ms36242/114, Ms364242/116, Ms36242/117, Ms36242/120, Ms36242/122, Ms36242/123, Ms36242/165, Ms36242/166, Ms36242/169, Ms36242/170, Ms36242/172, Ms36242/175, Ms36242/176, Ms36242/181, Ms36242/195, Ms36242/198, Ms36242/199, Ms36242/222, Ms36242/223, Ms36242/245.
- Letters: Ms36242/150, Ms36242/151, Ms36242/155, Ms36242/156, Ms36242/157, Ms36242/157ii, Ms36242/159, Ms36242/162, Ms36242/163, Ms36242/164, Ms36242/168, Ms36242/170, Ms36244/15, Ms36244/16, Ms36244/19.
- Esperanto in Scotland: Ms36244/1, Ms36244/3 and Ms36244/5. Meeting minutes, conference programmes and documents concerning Esperanto clubs and congresses: Ms38908/13, Ms38908/15, Ms38908/16.
- Biographical notes on John Beveridge: Ms36244/15.
- Articles, lectures and sermons in Esperanto and/or concerning Esperanto: Ms36244/2, Ms36244/4.
- Collection of Esperanto learning materials: Bev PM8202.E8; Bev PM8213.E8R7; Bev PM8213.C7; Bev PM8285.D6A5.
- Collection of Esperanto periodicals: Bev PM8201.S7B.

Periodicals

Allgemeine Zeitung (Frankfurt, 1850–present)
Amerika Esperantisto (Chicago/Washington DC/New York, 1906–67)
The British Esperantist (London/Barlaston, 1905–present)
Belga Esperantisto (Antwerp, 1908–14, 1920–40, 1945–61)
Bulgara Esperantisto (Sofia, 1919–present)
The Daily News (London, 1846–1930)
Dia Regno (Mühlheim, 1909–present)
Dundee Courier (later *The Courier*) (Dundee, 1801–present)

Evening Standard (later *The London Standard*) (London, 1827–present)
Fervoja Esperantisto (Paris, 1910–14)
Finna Esperantisto (Helsinki, 1907–10, 1912–14)
Internacia Scienca Revuo (Paris/Geneva/Kötzschenbroda/Horrem, 1904–23)
Nica Literatura Revuo (Choisy-le-Roi, 1955–62)
Norsk Tidend (London, 1940–45)
The Perthshire Advertiser (Perth, 1829–present)
Le Progrès (Lyon, 1859–present)
La Revuo (Paris, 1906–14)
Oficiala Gazeto Esperantista (Geneva, 1908–1922)
The Times (London, 1785–present)
The Washington Herald (Washington DC, 1906–39)

Printed primary sources

Baghy, Julio. *Preter la Vivo*. Budapest: Literatura Mondo, 1922.

Baird, Jane, William Harvey and John Mabon Warden. *The Edinburgh Esperanto Pocket Dictionary*. Edinburgh: Thomas Nelson and Sons, 1915.

Beveridge, Heather. 'Hidro de para-toluidino', *Internacia Science Revuo* 5 (1908), 7–11.

Beveridge, John. *La Prediko sur la Monto*. Edinburgh: Andrew Elliot, 1910.

Boirac, Émile. *Plena Vortaro Esperanto-Esperanta kaj Esperanto-Franca. Unua Parto*. Dijon: Darantière, 1909.

Boirac, Émile. *Plena Vortaro Esperanto-Esperanta kaj Esperanto-Franca. Dua Parto*. Dijon: Darantière, 1910.

British Esperanto Association. *Esperanto for All: How to Read, Write and Speak It*. London: British Esperanto Association, 1913.

British Esperanto Association. *Esperanto for Beginners*. London: British Esperanto Association, n.d.

Brzostowksi, Aleksander Bolesław, ed. *Adresaro de Polaj Esperantistoj por 1909*. Warsaw: Jan Günther, 1909.

Bujwidowa, Kazimiera. *Kwestya kobieca: czy kobieta powinna mieć te same prawa co mężczyzna?* Kraków: nakł. Towarzystwo Wydawniczego 'Encyklopedyi Ludowej', 1909.

Carroll, Lewis. *La aventuroj de Alico en Mirlando*. Translated by E. L. Kearney. London: British Esperanto Association, 1910.

Couturat, Louis, and Léopold Leau. *Histoire de la Langue Universelle*. Paris: Hachette, 1903.

Couturat, Louis, and Léopold Leau. *Les Nouvelles Langues Internationales: Suite à l'Histoire de la Langue Universelle*. Paris: Hachette, 1907.

Couturat, Louis, Otto Jespersen, Richard Lorenz, Leopold Pfaundler Von Hadermur and Wilhelm Ostwald. *International Language and Science: Considerations on the Introduction of an International Language into Science*. London: Constable and Company Limited, 1910.

Cox, George. *A Grammar and Commentary on the International Language Esperanto*. London: British Esperanto Association, 1914.

Drezen, Ernest. *Zamenhof*. Leipzig: Sennacieca Asocio Tutmonda, 1929.

Esperantista Centra Oficejo. *Kvara Universala Kongreso de Esperanto*. Paris: Esperantista Centra Oficejo, 1909.

Esperantista Centra Oficejo. *Sepa Universala Kongreso de Esperanto*. Paris: Esperantista Centra Oficejo, 1912.

Fruictier, Paul. *Esperanta sintakso laŭ verkoj de S-ro D-ro Zamenhof kaj aliaj aŭtoroj*. Paris: Hachette, 1907.

Gesellschaft Esperanto Dresden. Dresden: Gebr. Arnhold, 1910.

Glück, Julius. *La Jubilea Kongreso de Esperanto 1912: Rememoraĵoj kaj oficialaj dokumentoj*. Purmerend: J. Muusses, 1912.

Goethe, Johann Wolfgang von. *Ifigenio en Taŭrido: Dramo en kvin aktoj*. Translated by Ludwik Lejzer Zamenhof. Paris: Hachette, 1908.

Hankel, Marie. *Sableroj*. Leipzig: Deutsche Esperanto Buchhandlung, 1911.

Levertin, Oskar. 'Shylock. Poemo de O. Levertin, esperantigis Hj. J. Runeberg', *Finna Esperantisto*, 1909.

Libro de la Sesa Internacia Kongreso: Aŭgusto 14a–20a. Washington, DC: La Kongreso, 1910.

Ménil, Félicien de, ed. *Tutmonda Jarlibro Esperantista Enhavanta La Adresaron de Dro Zamenhof por 1904*. Paris: Hachette, 1904.

Ménil, Félicien de, ed. *Tutmonda Jarlibro Esperantista Enhavanta La Adresaron de Dro Zamenhof por 1907*. Paris: Hachette, 1907.

Ménil, Félicien de, ed. *Tutmonda Jarlibro Esperantista Enhavanta la Adresaron de Dro Zamenhof por 1909*. Paris: Hachette, 1909.

Mielck, W. B., and F. Stephan, trans. *La Evangelio Sankta Mateo laŭ Dro Martin Luther*. Leipzig: J. C. Hinrich'sche Buchhandlung, 1906.

Newspaper clippings 1898–1915, Austrian National Library, www.onb.ac.at/en/departments/department-of-planned-languages/digital-collections/newspaper-clippings-1898-1915

Neumark, E., trans. *La Libro Ruth*. Nürnberg: Presejo de W. Tümmel, 1893.

La Nova Testamento de nia Sinjoro kaj Savanto Jesuo Kristo. London: La Brita kaj Eksterlanda Biblia Societo / Edinburgh and Glasgow: Nacia Biblia Societo de Skotlando, 1912.

Orzeszkowa, Eliza. *Kilka słów o kobietach*. Lwów: Rogosz, 1873.

Orzeszkowa, Eliza. *Marta*. Warsaw: S. Lewentala, 1885.

Report of Commission I: Carrying the Gospel to All the Non-Christian World; with Supplement: Presentation and Discussion of the Report in the Conference on 15th June 1910. Edinburgh: Publ. for the World Missionary Conference by Oliphant, Anderson & Ferrier, 1910.

Report of Commission II: The Church in the Mission Field. Edinburgh: Publ. for the World Missionary Conference by Oliphant, Anderson & Ferrier, 1910.

Robbie, James. *The Esperanto Home-Student*. Edinburgh: Leith Burghs Pilot, 1913.

Royal Society for the Encouragement of Arts, Manufactures and Commerce. 'List of the Council and Officers for the 145th Session, 1898–9', *The Journal of the Society of Arts* 47, no. 2400 (1898): 1–44.

Rust, John Cyprian. *Ordo de Diservo, Laŭ la Preĝlibro de la Angla Eklezio*. London: La Tria Kongreso, 1907.

Sächsisches Esperanto-Institut Dresden, ed. *Bericht*. Dresden: Druckerei des Esperanto-Verlages F. Emil Boden, 1908.

Salokannel, Hugo William. *Biografiaro de l'Parencaro Salokannel*. Vaasa: Ikka, 1952.

La Sankta Biblio: Malnova kaj Nova Testamentoj tradukitaj el la originalaj lingvoj. London: Brita kaj Alilanda Biblio Societo / Edinburgh and Glasgow: Nacia Biblia Societo de Skotlando, 1926.

Schleyer, Johann Martin. *Pened balid Yoliánesà*. Konstanz: VOL, 1888.

Scotland Census, 1911, National Records of Scotland, Ref: 282/18/5, '1911, Beveridge, John'. https://www.scotlandspeople.gov.uk/ (accessed 20 July 2021).

Scotland Census, 1911, National Records of Scotland, Ref: 685/2 44/ 20, '1911 Simpson, Lucy May'. https://www.scotlandspeople.gov.uk (accessed 20 July 2021).

Universala Kongreso de Esperanto. *2a Universala Kongreso de Esperanto: Nomaro de la kongresanoj*. Geneva: Universala Kongreso de Esperanto, 1907.

Wackrill, Alfred E. *Kelkaj Impresoj de Hindujo. Literatura Almanako*. Paris: Presa Esperantista Societo, 1909.

Wilson, George B. 'A Statistical Review of the Variations during the Last Twenty Years in the Consumption of Intoxicating Drinks in the United Kingdom, and in Convictions for Offences Connected with Intoxication, with Discussion of the Causes to which these Variations may be Ascribed', *Journal of the Royal Statistical Society* 75, no. 2 (1912): 183–247.

Wilson, George Bailey. *Alcohol and the Nation: A Contribution to the Study of the Liquor Problem in the United Kingdom from 1800 to 1935*. London: Nicholson and Watson, 1940.

Zamenhof, Ludwik Lejzer. *Adresaro de la Personoj, Kiuj Ellernis la Lingvon 'Esperanto'*. Warsaw: Zamenhof, 1889.

Zamenhof, Ludwik Lejzer. *Dr. Esperanto's International Language: Introduction and Complete Grammar*. Warsaw: Zamenhof, 1887.

Zamenhof, Ludwik Lejzer. *Fundamento de Esperanto*. Paris: Hachette, 1905.

Zamenhof, Ludwik Lejzer. *Fundamenta Krestomatio de la Lingvo Esperanto*. Paris: Hachette, 1905.

Zamenhof, Ludwig Lejzer. 'Paroladoj: Tria Kongreso 1907 en Cambridge', in *Originala Verkaro de L. L. Zamenhof*, edited by Johannes Dietterle, 374–381. Leipzig: Ferdinand Hirt & Sohn, 1929.

Zamenhof, Ludwik Lejzer. *La Psalmaro el la Biblio. El la originalo tradukis d-ro L. L. Zamenhof*. Paris: Hachette, 1908.

Zamenhof, Ludwig Lejzer. 'Al Pastro J. Cyprian Rust, "Pri la Malnova Testamento"', in *Originala Verkaro de L. L. Zamenhof*, edited by Johannes Dietterle, 472. Leipzig: Ferdinand Hirt & Sohn, 1929.

Zamenhof, Ludwik Lejzer, Gerrit Berveling, John Cyprian Rust, John Beveridge and C. G. Wilkinson, trans. *Biblio*. Dobřichovice: Kava-Pech, 2006.

Secondary literature

Alcalde, Ángel. 'Spatializing Transnational History: European Spaces and Territories'. *European Review of History: Revue Européenne d'Histoire* 25, nos. 3–4 (2018): 553–67. https://doi.org/10.1080/13507486.2018.1439885.

Alcalde, Javier. *Esperanto i Anarquisme: Els Orígens (1887–1907)*. Barcelona: Edicions Malcriàs d'Agràcia, 2022.

Alcalde, Javier. 'Pioneers of Internationalism: Esperanto and the First World War', in *Multilingual Environments in the Great War*, ed. Julian Walker and Christophe Declercq (London: Bloomsbury, 2021), 44–57.

Aldridge, Frederick. *The Development of the Wycliffe Bible Translators and the Summer Institute of Linguistics, 1934–1982*. PhD dissertation, University of Stirling, 2012.

Allen, Ann Taylor, and Anne Cova. 'Introduction: Transnational Women's Activism'. *Women's History Review* 32, no. 2 (2023): 165–71. https://doi.org/10.1080/09612025.2022.2100566.

Anderson, Benedict. *Imagined Communities: Reflections on the Origin and Spread of Nationalism*. London: Verso, 1991.

Anderson, Michael. *Scotland's Populations from the 1850s to Today*. Oxford: Oxford University Press, 2018.

Andriotis, Konstantinos and Mišela Mavrič. 'Postcard Mobility: Going Beyond Image and Text'. *Annals of Tourism Research* 40, no. 1 (2013): 18–39. https://doi.org/10.1016/j.annals.2012.07.004.

Askew, Thomas A. 'The New York 1900 Ecumenical Missionary Conference: A Centennial Reflection'. *International Bulletin of Missionary Research* 24, no. 4 (2000): 146–54.

Bartley, Paula. *Emmeline Pankhurst*. London: Routledge, 2002.

Barton, David, and Mary Hamilton. *Local Literacies: Reading and Writing in One Community*. London: Routledge, 2012.

Beauchamp, K. G. *Exhibiting Electricity*. London: The Institution of Electrical Engineers, 1997.

Benedict, Burton. *The Anthropology of World's Fairs: San Francisco's Panama Pacific International Exposition of 1915*. Berkeley: Lowie Museum of Anthropology and Scolar Press, 1983.

Bernal, John Desmond. *Science in History, Volume 2: The Scientific and Industrial Revolution*. London: Penguin Books, 1965.

Blom, Philipp. *The Vertigo Years: Change and Culture in the West, 1900–1914*. London: Weidenfeld & Nicolson, 2008.

Borsboom, Ed. *Vivo de Lanti*. Paris: Sennacieca Asocio Tutmonda, 1976.

Boulton, Marjorie. *Zamenhof: Creator of Esperanto*. London: Routledge and Kegan Paul, 1960.

Branca, Patricia. *Silent Sisterhood: Middle-Class Women in the Victorian Home*. London: Routledge, 2012.

Brown, Heloise. *'The Truest Form of Patriotism': Pacifist Feminism in Britain, 1870–1902*. Manchester: Manchester University Press, 2003.

Brydan, David, and Jessica Reinisch, eds. *Internationalists in European History: Rethinking the Twentieth Century*. New York: Bloomsbury Academic, 2021.

Burghelea, Manuela. 'On Not Being Lost in Translation: Creative Strategies to Approach Multiculturalism in Esperanto'. *Język, Komunikacja, Informacja* 13 (2018): 159–74. https://doi.org/10.14746/jki.2018.13.11.

Caligaris, Irene. *Unu Lingvo por Ĉiuj, Unu Lingvo de Neniu Lando: Surkampa Esploro pri la Esperantaj Identecoj*. Pisa: Edistudio, 2021.

Centassi, René, and Henri Masson. *L'Homme qui a Défié Babel: Ludwig Lejzer Zamenhof*. Paris: Harmattan, 1995.

Chakrabarty, Dipesh. *The Calling of History*. Chicago: University of Chicago Press, 2015.

Clavin, Patricia. 'Defining Transnationalism'. *Contemporary European History* 14, no. 4 (2005): 421–39. https://doi.org/10.1017/S0960777305002705.

Connelly, John. *From Peoples into Nations: A History of Eastern Europe*. Princeton: Princeton University Press, 2020.

Conrad, Sebastian. *Globalisation and the Nation in Imperial Germany*. Cambridge: Cambridge University Press, 2010.

Creusot, Thomas. *L'Utopie sous Presse: Éditer l'Espéranto en France (1897–1939)*. Master's dissertation, École nationale des chartes, 2022.

Davis, Natalie Zemon. 'Decentering History: Local Stories and Cultural Crossings in a Global World'. *History and Theory* 50, no. 2 (2011): 188–202. https://doi.org/10.1111/j.1468-2303.2011.00576.x.

Delap, Lucy. *Feminisms: A Global History*. Chicago: University of Chicago Press, 2020.

Delap, Lucy. *The Feminist Avant-Garde: Transatlantic Encounters of the Early Twentieth Century*. Cambridge: Cambridge University Press, 2009.

Dennison, Patricia. *The Evolution of Scotland's Towns: Creation, Growth and Fragmentation*. Edinburgh: Edinburgh University Press, 2022.

Duranti, Alessandro. *Linguistic Anthropology*. Cambridge: Cambridge University Press, 1997.

Eco, Umberto. *The Search for the Perfect Language*. Oxford: Blackwell Publishers, 1995.

England, Kim, and Kate Boyer. 'Women's Work: The Feminization and Shifting Meanings of Clerical Work'. *Journal of Social History* 43, no. 2 (2009): 307–40. https://doi.org/10.1353/jsh.0.0284.

Fettes, Mark. 'The Lady, the Linguists, and the International Language'. *Language Problems and Language Planning* 25, no. 2 (2001): 177–84. https://doi.org/10.1075/lplp.25.2.06fet.

Fians, Guilherme. 'Bringing Constructed Languages Back to the Debate: The Contributions of Interlinguistics to General Linguistics'. *Investigationes Linguisticae* 46 (2022): 43–52. https://doi.org/10.14746/il.2022.46.5.

Fians, Guilherme. *Esperanto Revolutionaries and Geeks: Language Politics, Digital Media and the Making of an International Community.* Cham: Palgrave Macmillan, 2021.

Fians, Guilherme, 'La Kosmopolito kaj la Aliulo: Historiaj konsideroj pri diferenco kaj diverseco laŭ la vidpunkto de esperantistoj', in *En la mondon venis nova lingvo: Festlibro por la 75-jariĝo de Ulrich Lins*, ed. Hitosi Gotoo, Goro Christoph Kimura and José Antonio Vergara, 475–95 (New York: Mondial, 2018).

Fians, Guilherme. 'Mind the Age Gap: Communication Technologies and Intergenerational Language Transmission among Esperanto Speakers in France'. *Language Problems and Language Planning* 44, no. 1 (2020): 87–108. https://doi.org/10.1075/lplp.00057.fia.

Fians, Guilherme. 'Neutralizing the Political: Language Ideology as Censorship in Esperanto Youth Media during the Cold War'. *Journal of Linguistic Anthropology* 34, no. 2 (2024), 200–219. https://doi.org/10.1111/jola.12427.

Fians, Guilherme, 'O que falar em esperanto quer dizer: Revisitando políticas prefigurativas, movimentos sociais e as novas esquerdas Mana'. *Estudos de Antropologia Social* 29, no. 1 (2023): 1–31.

Fians, Guilherme, 'TEJO, um maduro movimento de juventude', 240–53, in *O Esperanto Alem da Lingua*, ed. Fernando Pita and Guilherme Fians. Porto Velho: Temática, 2017.

Fiedler, Sabine. 'Standardization and Self-Regulation in an International Speech Community: The Case of Esperanto'. *International Journal of the Sociology of Language* 177 (2006): 67–90. https://doi.org/10.1515/IJSL.2006.005.

Fischer-Tiné, Harald, Stefan Huebner and Ian R. Tyrrell, eds. *Spreading Protestant Modernity: Global Perspectives on the Social Work of the YMCA and YWCA, 1889–1970*. Honolulu: University of Hawai'i Press, 2021.

Forster, Peter G. *The Esperanto Movement: Contributions to the Sociology of Language*. The Hague: Mouton, 1982.

Freedman, Estelle B. 'The New Woman: Changing Views of Women in the 1920s'. *The Journal of American History* 61, no. 2 (1974): 372–93. https://doi.org/10.2307/1903954.

Fumurescu, Ana. *Visualizing Agency: Postcards and Romanian National Identity*. Bloomington, IN: Indiana University Press, 2015.

Gardey, Delphine. 'Mechanizing Writing and Photographing the Word: Utopias, Office Work, and Histories of Gender and Technology'. *History and Technology* 17, no. 4 (2001): 319–52. https://doi.org/10.1080/07341510108581999.

Gardey, Delphine. 'The Standardization of a Technical Practice: Typing (1883–1930)'. *History and Technology* 15, no. 4 (1999): 313–43. https://doi.org/10.1080/07341519908581951.

Garvía, Roberto. *Esperanto and Its Rivals: The Struggle for an International Language*. Philadelphia: University of Pennsylvania Press, 2015.

Garvía, Roberto. *Lengua y Utopia: El Movimiento Esperantista en España (1890–1936)*. Granada: Editorial Universidad de Granada, 2021.

Gauldie, Enid. 'The Dundee Jute Industry', in *Scottish Textile History*, edited by John Butt and Kenneth Ponting, 112–25. Aberdeen: Aberdeen University Press, 1987.

Gelber, Steven M. 'Free Market Metaphor: The Historical Dynamics of Stamp Collecting'. *Comparative Studies in Society and History* 4, no. 34 (1992): 742–69. https://doi.org/10.1017/S0010417500018077.

Gillen, Julia, and Nigel Hall. 'Edwardian Postcards: Illuminating Ordinary Writing', in *The Anthropology of Writing: Understanding Textually Mediated Worlds*, edited by David Barton and Uta Papen, 169–89. London: Bloomsbury, 2012.

Goodall, Grant. 'Constructed Languages'. *Annual Review of Linguistics* 9 (2023): 419–37. https://doi.org/10.1146/annurev-linguistics-030421-064707.

Gordin, Michael. *Scientific Babel: How Science Was Done Before and After Global English*. Chicago: University of Chicago Press, 2015.

Gordon, Eleanor. *Women and the Labour Movement in Scotland 1850–1914*. Oxford: Oxford University Press, 1991.

Greatex, Geoffrey. 'Translations of Virgil into Esperanto', in *Virgil and His Translators*, edited by Susanna Braund and Zara Martirosova Torlone, 124–35. Oxford: Oxford University Press, 2018.

Greble, Emily. *Muslims and the Making of Modern Europe*. Oxford: Oxford University Press, 2021.

Green, Abigail, and Vincent Viaene, eds. *Religious Internationals in the Modern World: Globalization and Faith Communities since 1750*. Basingstoke: Palgrave Macmillan, 2012.

Gregor, Douglas Bartlett. *La Esperanta Traduko de la Malnova Testamento: Dek-Biblia Konkordanco de 518 Diskutindaj Versoj*. Scheveningen: Heroldo de Esperanto, 1958.

Grieves, Kevin. 'Esperanto Journalism and Readers as "Managers": A Transnational Participatory Audience'. *Media History* 27, no. 1 (2020): 1–13. https://doi.org/10.1080/13688804.2020.1727319.

Halperin, Liora. 'Other Tongues: The Place of Foreign Language in Hebrew Culture', in *Reflections on Knowledge and Language in Middle Eastern Societies*, edited by Bruno de Nicola, Yonatan Mendel and Husain Qutbuddin, 228–47. Newcastle upon Tyne: Cambridge Scholars Publishing, 2010.

Handman, Courtney. *Critical Christianity: Translation and Denominational Conflict in Papua New Guinea*. Oakland: University of California Press, 2015.

Heller, Wendy. *Lidia: The Life of Lidia Zamenhof, the Daughter of Esperanto*. Oxford: George Ronald, 1985.

Hobsbawm, Eric. *The Age of Empire, 1875–1914*. New York: Vintage Books, 1989.

Hoppen, K. Theodore. *The Mid-Victorian Generation, 1846–1886*. London: Clarendon Press, 1998.

Hughes-Johnson, Alexandra, and Lyndsey Jenkins, eds. *The Politics of Women's Suffrage: Local, National and International Dimensions*. London: University of London Press, 2021.

Hunt, Karen. 'Suffrage Internationalism in Practice: Dora Montefiore and the Lessons of Finnish Women's Enfranchisement', in *The Politics of Women's Suffrage: Local, National and International Dimensions*, edited by Alexandra Hughes-Johnson and Lyndsey Jenkins, 285–308. London: University of London Press, 2021.

Jaffe, Alexandra. *Ideologies in Action: Language Politics on Corsica*. Berlin: Mouton De Gruyter, 1999.

James, Kevin J., Melissa McAfee, Aritra Bhattacharjee, Alexandra Kurceba and Ainsley Robertson. 'Greetings from Scotland: Postcards and the Digitisation of Travel Ephemera in the University of Guelph's Scottish Collections'. *The International Review of Scottish Studies* 44 (2019): 3–9. https://doi.org/10.21083/irss.v44i0.5836.

Jordanova, Ludmilla. *History in Practice*. London: Bloomsbury, 2019.

Kamarýt, Stanisłav. *Historio de la Esperanto-Movado en Ĉehoslovakio: Iom da Historio kaj iom da Rememoroj*. Prague: Ĉeha Esperanto-Asocio, 1983.

Kamenov, Nikolay. *Global Temperance and the Balkans: American Missionaries, Swiss Scientists and Bulgarian Socialists, 1870–1940*. Cham: Palgrave Macmillan, 2020.

Keane, Webb. *Christian Moderns: Freedom and Fetish in the Mission Encounter*. Berkeley: University of California Press, 2007.

Kemp, John. 'Red Tayside? Political Change in Early Twentieth-Century Dundee', in Christopher A. Whatley and Bob Harris, eds. *Victorian Dundee: Image and Realities*, 217–39. East Linton: Tuckwell, 2000.

Kökény, Lajos, and Vilmos Bleier, eds. *Enciklopedio de Esperanto*. Budapest: Literatura Mondo, 1933.

Kołodziejska-Smagała, Zuzanna. 'Polish-Jewish Female Writers and the Women's Emancipation Movements in the Late Nineteenth and Early Twentieth Centuries'. *Aspasia*, 16 (2022): 110–29. https://doi.org/10.3167/asp.2022.160108.

Korzhenkov, Aleksandr. *Zamenhof: The Life, Works, and Ideas of the Author of Esperanto*. New York: Mondial, 2010.

Koschek, Marcel. 'TEKA: A Transnational Network of Esperanto-Speaking Physicians'. *Hungarian Historical Review* 10, no. 2 (2021): 243–66. https://doi.org/10.38145/2021.2.243.

Kreuder-Sonnen, Katharina. 'From Transnationalism to Olympic Internationalism: Polish Medical Experts and International Scientific Exchange, 1885–1939'. *Contemporary European History* 25, no. 2 (2016): 207–31. https://doi.org/10.1017/S0960777316000047.

Kwolek-Folland, Angel. *Engendering Business: Men and Women in the Corporate Office, 1870–1930*. Baltimore, MD: Johns Hopkins University Press, 1994.

Lake, Robert. 'Gender and Etiquette in British Lawn Tennis 1870–1939: A Case Study of "Mixed Doubles."' *The International Journal of the*

History of Sport 29, no. 5 (2012): 691–710. https://doi.org/10.1080/09523367.2012.675203.

Langland, Elizabeth. *Nobody's Angels: Middle-Class Women and Domestic Ideology in Victorian Culture*. Ithaca, NY: Cornell University Press, 1995.

Ledger, Sally. *The New Woman: Fiction and Feminism at the Fin de Siècle*. Manchester: Manchester University Press, 1997.

Lenman, Bruce, Charlotte Lythe and Enid Gauldie. *Dundee and Its Textile Industry, 1850–1914*. Dundee: Abertay Historical Society, 1969.

Limor, Yehiel, and Ilan Tamir. 'The Neglected Medium: Postage Stamps as Mass Media'. *Communication Theory* 31, no. 3 (2021): 491–505. https://doi.org/10.1093/ct/qtz043.

Lins, Ulrich. *La Danĝera Lingvo: Esperanto en la Uragano de Persekutoj*. Kyoto: L'Omnibuso, 1973.

Lins, Ulrich. *Dangerous Language: Esperanto and the Decline of Stalinism*. London: Palgrave Macmillan, 2017.

Lins, Ulrich. *Dangerous Language: Esperanto under Hitler and Stalin*. London: Palgrave Macmillan, 2016.

Lowe, Graham. *Women in the Administrative Revolution: The Feminization of Clerical Work*. Toronto: University of Toronto Press, 1987.

Lynch, Michael. 'John Knox, Minister of Edinburgh and Commissioner of the Kirk', in *John Knox and the British Reformations*, edited by Roger Mason, 242–67. London: Routledge, 2018.

Lyons, John. *Introduction to Theoretical Linguistics*. Cambridge: Cambridge University Press, 1968.

Macdonald, Murdo. 'The Patron, the Professor and the Painter: Cultural Activity in Dundee at the Close of the Nineteenth Century', in *Victorian Dundee: Image and Realities*, edited by Christopher A. Whatley and Bob Harris, 197–216. East Linton: Tuckwell Press, 2000.

Marcus, George E. 'Ethnography in/of the World System: The Emergence of Multi-Sited Ethnography'. *Annual Review of Anthropology* 24 (1995): 95–117. https://doi.org/10.1146/annurev.an.24.100195.000523.

Markov, Anne-Sophie. *Le Mouvement International des Travailleurs Espérantistes, 1918–1939*. Master's dissertation, Université de Versailles Saint-Quentin-en-Yvelines, 1999.

Masuzawa, Tomoko. *The Invention of World Religions or How European Universalism Was Preserved in the Language of Pluralism*. Chicago: University of Chicago Press, 2005.

Matthias, Ulrich. *Esperanto: La Nova Latino de la Eklezio*. Antwerp: Flandra Esperanto-Ligo, 2002.

Metzger, Bruce. *The Bible in Translation: Ancient and English Versions*. Grand Rapids, MI: Baker Academic, 2001.

Metzger, Bruce. *The Text of the New Testament: Its Transmission, Corruption, and Restoration*. Oxford: Oxford University Press, 1968.

Metzger, Bruce. *A Textual Commentary on the Greek New Testament*. London and New York: United Bible Societies, 1971.

Müller, Simone. *Wiring the World: The Social and Cultural Creation of Global Telegraph Networks*. New York: Columbia University Press, 2016.

Neuburger, Mary. *The Orient Within: Muslim Minorities and the Negotiation of Nationhood in Modern Bulgaria*. Ithaca, NY: Cornell University Press, 2011.

Nitobe, Inazô. 'Esperanto and the Language Question at the League of Nations', in *Al Lingva Demokratio / Towards Linguistic Democracy / Vers La Démocratie Linguistique*, edited by Mark Fettes and Suzanne Bolduc, 62–78. Rotterdam: Universala Esperanto-Asocio, 1998.

Noworolska, Barbara. *Eliza Orzeszkowa. Trwanie, pamięć, historia*. Białystok: Wydawnictwo Uniwersytetu w Białymstoku, 2005.

Offen, Karen M. *European Feminisms, 1700–1950: A Political History*. Stanford, CA: Stanford University Press, 2000.

O'Keeffe, Brigid. *Esperanto and Languages of Internationalism in Revolutionary Russia*. London: Bloomsbury Academic, 2021.

O'Keeffe, Brigid. 'An International Language for an Empire of Humanity: L. L. Zamenhof and The Imperial Russian Origins of Esperanto'. *East European Jewish Affairs* 49, no. 1 (2019): 1–19. https://doi.org/10.1080/13501674.2019.1618165.

Oram, Alison. *Women Teachers and Feminist Politics, 1900–39*. Manchester: Manchester University Press, 1996.

Osterhammel, Jürgen. *The Transformation of the World: A Global History of the Nineteenth Century*. Princeton: Princeton University Press, 2014.

Pabst, Bernhard. *Marie Hankel (1844–1929): Esperanto-Dichterin, Organisatorin, Feministin*. Bonn: Selbstverlag, 2002.

Peltonen, Matti. 'Clues, Margins, and Monads: The Micro-Macro Link in Historical Research'. *History and Theory* 40, no. 3 (2001): 347–59. https://doi.org/10.1111/0018-2656.00172.

Phillipson, Robert. *Linguistic Imperialism*. Oxford: Oxford University Press, 1992.

Privat, Edmond. *La Vivo de Zamenhof.* Tyresö: Inko, 2001.

Prochaska, David, and Jordana Mendelson, eds. *Postcards: Ephemeral Histories of Modernity.* University Park: Pennsylvania State University Press, 2010.

Purvis, June. 'Emmeline Pankhurst (1858–1928), Suffragette Leader and Single Parent in Edwardian Britain'. *Women's History Review* 20, no. 1 (2011): 87–108. https://doi.org/10.1080/09612025.2011.536389.

Rapley, Ian. *Green Star Japan: Esperanto and the International Language Question, 1880–1945* (Honolulu, HI: University of Hawai'i Press, 2024).

Rapley, Ian. 'Talking to the World: Esperanto and Popular Internationalism in Prewar Japan'. *Japan Society Proceedings* 152 (2016): 76–89.

Rapley, Ian. 'Sekaigo: Esperanto, International Language, and the Transnational Dimension to Japan's Linguistic Modernity'. *Japan Forum* 32, no. 4 (2020): 511–30. https://doi.org/10.1080/09555803.2019.1594342.

Rašić, Nikola. *La Rondo Familia: Sociologiaj Esploroj en Esperantio.* Pisa: Edistudio, 1994.

Rayner-Canham, Marelene, and Geoffrey Rayner-Canham. *Chemistry Was Their Life: Pioneering British Women Chemists, 1880–1949.* London: Imperial College Press, 2008.

Reinisch, Jessica. 'Introduction: Agents of Internationalism'. *Contemporary European History* 25, no. 2 (2016): 195–205. https://doi.org/10.1017/S0960777316000035.

Revel, Jacques. *Jeux d'echelles: la micro-analyse à l'expérience*, edited by Jacques Revel. Paris: Gallimard Le Seuil, 1996.

Richmond, Ian. 'Esperanto Literature and the International Reader', in *Aspects of Internationalism: Language and Culture*, edited by Ian Richmond, 103–18. Lanham, MD: University Press of America, 1993.

Rodogno, Davide, Bernhard Struck, and Jakob Vogel, eds. *Shaping the Transnational Sphere: Experts, Networks and Issues from the 1840s to the 1930s*. New York: Berghahn, 2014.

Rogan, Bjarne. 'An Entangled Object: The Picture Postcard as Souvenir and Collectible, Exchange and Ritual Communication'. *Cultural Analysis* 4 (2005): 1–27.

Rüger, Jan. 'OXO: Or, the Challenges of Transnational History'. *European History Quarterly* 40, no. 4 (2010): 656–68. https://doi.org/10.1177/0265691410376488.

Rupp, Leila J. 'Constructing Internationalism: The Case of Transnational Women's Organizations, 1888–1945', *The American Historical Review* 99, no. 5 (1994): 1571–1600. https://doi.org/10.1086/ahr/99.5.1571.

Rupp, Leila J. *Worlds of Women: The Making of an International Women's Movement*. Princeton: Princeton University Press, 1997.

Sarafov, Ivan. *Skizo de la Historio de Bulgara Esperanto-Movado*. Sofia: Bulgara Espeantista Asocio, 1971.

Saunier, Pierre-Yves. *Transnational History*. Basingstoke: Palgrave Macmillan, 2013.

Schor, Esther. *Bridge of Words: Esperanto and the Dream of a Universal Language*. New York: Metropolitan Books / Henry Holt and Company, 2016.

Sethia, Tara. 'The Rise of the Jute Manufacturing Industry in Colonial India: A Global Perspective', *Journal of World History* 7, no. 1 (1996): 71–99. https://doi.org/10.1353/jwh.2005.0058.

Shackleton, Ken. 'Gender Segregation in Scottish Chartered Accountancy: The Deployment of Male Concerns about the Admission of Women, 1900–25'. *Accounting, Business & Financial History* 9, no. 1 (1999): 135–56. https://doi.org/10.1080/095852099330395.

Sikosek, Ziko Marcus. *Sed Homoj kun Homoj: Universalaj Kongresoj de Esperanto, 1905–2005*. Rotterdam: Universala Esperanto-Asocio, 2005.

Sluga, Glenda. *Internationalism in the Age of Nationalism*. Philadelphia: University of Pennsylvania Press, 2013.

Sluga, Glenda, and Patricia Clavin, eds. *Internationalisms: A Twentieth-Century History*. Cambridge: Cambridge University Press, 2016.

Smalley, William Allen. *Translation as Mission: Bible Translation in the Modern Missionary Movement*. Macon, GA: Mercer University Press, 1991.

Smith, Graham R. *'The Making of a Woman's Town': Household and Gender in Dundee, 1890–1940*. PhD thesis, University of Stirling, 1996.

Smith, John T. 'Russian Military Censorship during the First World War'. *Revolutionary Russia* 14, no. 1 (2001): 71–95. https://doi.org/10.1080/09546540108575734.

Stahl, Michael J. *The 'God of Israel' in History and Tradition*. Leiden: Brill, 2021.

Stanley, Brian. *The World Missionary Conference, Edinburgh 1910*. Grand Rapids, MI: William B. Eerdmans, 2009.

Stanley, Brian. 'Scotland and the World Missionary Conference, Edinburgh 1910', *Records of the Scottish Church History Society* 41 (2012): 113–32.

Stoll, David. 'The Summer Institute of Linguistics and Indigenous Movements'. *Latin American Perspectives* 9, no. 2 (1982), 84–99. https://doi.org/10.1177/0094582X8200900205.

Strom, Sharon Hartman. *Beyond the Typewriter: Gender, Class, and the Origins of Modern American Office Work, 1900–1930*. Urbana: University of Illinois Press, 1992.

Struck, Bernhard. 'Licht und Schatten im Esperantoland ohne Grenzen. Ein blinder Junge aus der Provinz, ein Eskimochef aus Mähren, ein Übersetzer aus England und Anarchisten in China', in *ZwischenWelten. Grenzüberschreitungen europäischer Geschichte*, edited by Katja Makhotina and Thomas Serrier, 269–82. Darmstadt: Wissenschaftliche Buchgesellschaft, 2023.

Struck, Bernhard. '(Plan)Sprachen und Wissen(-Sordnungen) um 1900', in *Wissen Ordnen und Entgrenzen—Vom Analogen Zum Digitalen Europa?*, edited by Joachim Berger and Thorsten Wübbena, 27–46. Göttingen: Vandenhoeck & Ruprecht, 2023.

Struck, Bernhard, Kate Ferris and Jacques Revel. 'Introduction: Space and Scale in Transnational History'. *The International History Review* 33, no. 4 (2011): 573–84. https://doi.org/10.1080/07075332.2011.620735.

Supu, Noo. *A Triglot Dictionary. Compiled by Dr. Ernest L. Richert and Ttopoqogo Hoopusus*. Ukarumpa: Summer Institute of Linguistics, 2002.

Sutton, Geoffrey. *Concise Encyclopedia of the Original Literature of Esperanto, 1887–2007*. New York: Mondial, 2008.

Thane, Pat. '"Well-Bred and Conventional Ladies": The National Council of Women of Great Britain and Ireland/Northern Ireland'. *Women's History Review* 32, no. 2 (2023): 172–89. https://doi.org/10.1080/09612025.2022.2100564.

Ther, Philipp. *Centre Stage: Operatic Culture and Nation Building in Nineteenth-Century Central Europe*. West Lafayette, IN: Purdue University Press, 2014.

Tomlinson, Jim. *Dundee and the Empire: 'Juteopolis' 1850–1939.* Edinburgh: Edinburgh University Press, 2016.

Tonkin, Humphrey. 'One Hundred Years of Esperanto: A Survey'. *Language Problems and Language Planning* 11, no. 3 (1987): 264–82. https://doi.org/10.1075/lplp.11.3.02ton.

Tonkin, Humphrey. *Lingvo kaj popolo: Aktualaj problemoj de la Esperanto-movado.* Rotterdam: Universala Esperanto-Asocio, 2006.

Tonkin, Humphrey. 'The Semantics of Invention: Translation into Esperanto', in *The Translator as Mediator of Cultures*, edited by Humphrey Tonkin and Maria Esposito Frank, 169–90. Amsterdam: John Benjamins, 2010.

Tyrrell, Ian. *Woman's World, Woman's Empire: The Woman's Christian Temperance Union in International Perspective, 1880–1930.* Chapel Hill: University of North Carolina, 1991.

Urla, Jacqueline. 'Ethnic Protest and Social Planning: A Look at Basque Language Revival'. *Cultural Anthropology* 3, no. 4 (1988): 379–94. https://doi.org/10.1525/can.1988.3.4.02a00030.

Velitchkova, Ana. 'Nationalized Cosmopolitanism with Communist Characteristics: The Esperanto Movement's Survival Strategy in Post–World War II Bulgaria'. *Social Science History* 46, no. 3 (2022): 617–42. https://doi.org/10.1017/ssh.2022.5.

Velitchkova, Ana. 'Rationalization of Belonging: Transnational Community Endurance', *International Sociology* 36, no. 3 (2021): 419–38. https://doi.org/10.1177/0268580920962005.

Vries, Jan de. 'Playing with Scales: The Global and the Micro, the Macro and the Nano'. *Past & Present* 242, no. 14 (2019): 23–36. https://doi.org/10.1093/pastj/gtz043.

Wainwright, Emma M. 'Constructing Gendered Workplace "Types": The Weaver-Millworker Distinction in Dundee's Jute Industry, c. 1880–1910'. *Gender, Place & Culture*, 14, no. 4 (2007): 467–9. https://doi.org/10.1080/09663690701439777.

Ware, Susan. *Why They Marched: Untold Stories of the Women Who Fought for the Right to Vote.* Cambridge, MA: Belknap Press, 2019.

Wells, John C. 'Esperanto', in *Encyclopedia of Language and Linguistics, Volume 4*, edited by Keith Brown, 223–5. New York: Elsevier, 2006.

Wenzlhuemer, Roland. 'The Dematerialization of Telecommunication: Communication Centres and Peripheries in Europe and the World,

1850–1920'. *Journal of Global History* 2, no. 3 (2007): 345–72. https://doi.org/10.1017/S174002280700232X.

Williamson, F. H. 'The International Postal Service and the Universal Postal Union'. *Journal of the Royal Institute of International Affairs* 9, no. 1 (1930): 68–78. https://doi.org/10.2307/3015625.

Wood, Richard E. 'A Voluntary Non-Ethnic, Non-Territorial Speech Community', in *Sociolinguistic Studies in Language Contact: Methods and Cases*, edited by William Francis Mackey and Jacob Ornstein, 433–50. The Hague: Mouton, 1979.

Young, Arlene. *From Spinster to Career Woman: Middle-Class Women and Work in Victorian England*. Montreal: McGill-Queen's Press, 2019.

Żelazny, Walter. *Ludwik Zamenhof: Life and Work. Reminiscences*. Białystok: Wydawnictwo Uniwersytetu w Białymstoku, 2020.

Index

www.ingramcontent.com/pod-product-compliance
Lightning Source LLC
LaVergne TN
LVHW052029300826
846742LV00025B/101